DELIVERANCE
AT DIEPHOLZ

The Stackpole Military History Series

THE AMERICAN CIVIL WAR
Cavalry Raids of the Civil War
In the Lion's Mouth
Witness to Gettysburg

WORLD WAR I
Doughboy War

WORLD WAR II
After D-Day
Airborne Combat
Armor Battles of the Waffen-SS,
    1943–45
Armoured Guardsmen
Arnhem 1944
The B-24 in China
The Battalion
The Battle of France
The Battle of Sicily
Battle of the Bulge, Vol. 1
Battle of the Bulge, Vol. 2
Battle of the Bulge, Vol. 3
Beyond the Beachhead
Beyond Stalingrad
The Black Bull
Blitzkrieg Unleashed
Blossoming Silk Against the Rising Sun
Bodenplatte
The Breaking Point
The Brigade
The Canadian Army and the Normandy
    Campaign
Clay Pigeons of St Lô, The
Critical Convoy Battles of WWII
A Dangerous Assignment
D-Day Bombers
D-Day Deception
D-Day to Berlin
Decision in the Ukraine
The Defense of Moscow 1941
Deliverance at Diepholz
Destination Normandy
Dive Bomber!
Eager Eagles
Eagles of the Third Reich
The Early Battles of Eighth Army
Eastern Front Combat
Europe in Flames
Exit Rommel
The Face of Courage
Fatal Decisions
Fist from the Sky
Flame On
Flying American Combat Aircraft of
    World War II, Vol. 1
For Europe
Forging the Thunderbolt
For the Homeland
Fortress France
The German Defeat in the East,
    1944–45
German Order of Battle, Vol. 1
German Order of Battle, Vol. 2
German Order of Battle, Vol. 3

The Germans in Normandy
Germany's Panzer Arm in World War II
GI Ingenuity
Goodbye, Transylvania
The Great Ships
Grenadiers
Guns Against the Reich
Hitler's Final Fortress
Hitler's Nemesis
Hitler's Spanish Legion
Hold the Westwall
Infantry Aces
In the Fire of the Eastern Front
Iron Arm
Iron Knights
Japanese Army Fighter Aces
Japanese Naval Fighter Aces
JG 26 Luftwaffe Fighter Wing War Diary,
    Vol. 1
JG 26 Luftwaffe Fighter Wing War Diary,
    Vol. 2
Kampfgruppe Peiper at the Battle of
    the Bulge
The Key to the Bulge
Kursk
Luftwaffe Aces
Luftwaffe Fighter Ace
Luftwaffe Fighter-Bombers over Britain
Luftwaffe Fighters & Bombers
Luftwaffe KG 200
Marshal of Victory, Vol. 1
Marshal of Victory, Vol. 2
Massacre at Tobruk
Mechanized Juggernaut or Military
    Anachronism?
Messerschmitts over Sicily
Michael Wittmann, Vol. 1
Michael Wittmann, Vol. 2
Mission 85
Mission 376
The Nazi Rocketeers
Night Flyer / Mosquito Pathfinder
No Holding Back
Operation Mercury
Panzer Aces
Panzer Aces II
Panzer Commanders of the
    Western Front
Panzergrenadier Aces
Panzer Gunner
The Panzer Legions
Panzers in Normandy
Panzers in Winter
Panzer Wedge, Vol. 1
Panzer Wedge, Vol. 2
The Path to Blitzkrieg
Penalty Strike
Poland Betrayed
Red Road from Stalingrad
Red Star Under the Baltic
Retreat to the Reich
Rommel Reconsidered
Rommel's Desert Commanders
Rommel's Desert War

Rommel's Lieutenants
The Savage Sky
The Seeds of Disaster
Ship-Busters
The Siege of Brest 1941
The Siege of Küstrin
The Siegfried Line
A Soldier in the Cockpit
Soviet Blitzkrieg
Spitfires & Yellow Tail Mustangs
Stalin's Keys to Victory
Surviving Bataan and Beyond
T-34 in Action
Tank Tactics
Tigers in the Mud
Triumphant Fox
The 12th SS, Vol. 1
The 12th SS, Vol. 2
Twilight of the Gods
Typhoon Attack
The War Against Rommel's Supply Lines
War in the Aegean
War of the White Death
Warsaw 1944
Winter Storm
The Winter War
Wolfpack Warriors
Zhukov at the Oder

THE COLD WAR / VIETNAM
Cyclops in the Jungle
Expendable Warriors
Fighting in Vietnam
Flying American Combat Aircraft:
    The Cold War
Here There Are Tigers
Jack of All Trades
Land with No Sun
Phantom Reflections
Street without Joy
Through the Valley
Tours of Duty
Two One Pony

**WARS OF AFRICA AND THE
MIDDLE EAST**
The Rhodesian War

GENERAL MILITARY HISTORY
Battle of Paoli
Cavalry from Hoof to Track
Desert Battles
Guerrilla Warfare
The Philadelphia Campaign, Vol. 1
Ranger Dawn
Sieges
The Spartan Army

DELIVERANCE AT DIEPHOLZ

A WWII Prisoner of War's Story

Jack Dower

STACKPOLE
BOOKS

Published by
STACKPOLE BOOKS
5067 Ritter Road
Mechanicsburg, PA 17055
www.stackpolebooks.com

Printed in the United States of America

10 9 8 7 6 5 4 3 2 1

First edition

Cover design by Wendy A. Reynolds
Cover photos from author's collection

Library of Congress Cataloging-in-Publication Data

Names: Dower, Jack, 1919–1984.
Title: Deliverance at Diepholz : a WWII prisoner of war's story / Jack Dower.
Description: First edition. | Mechanicsburg, PA : Stackpole Books, [2016] |
   Series: Stackpole military history series
Identifiers: LCCN 2015030155 | ISBN 9780811717533
Subjects: LCSH: Dower, Jack, 1919–1984. | United States. Army. Infantry
   Regiment, 179th. Company L—Biography. | Prisoners of war—United
   States—Biography. | Prisoners of war—Germany—Biography. | World War,
   1939–1945—Prisoners and prisons—Germany. | World War, 1939–1945—
   Personal narratives, American.
Classification: LCC D769.31 179th .D675 2016 | DDC 940.54/7243092—
dc23 LC record available at http://lccn.loc.gov/2015030155

This book is respectfully dedicated to the
World Red Cross Organization,
and particularly to the American Red Cross.
Without their food parcels,
thousands of Allied soldiers would never have survived.

Contents

Preface

Deliverance at Diepholz is an authentic account of the life of a prisoner of war deep in the heartland of Germany during 1944 and 1945. It does not purport to be a heroic tale. There are no accounts of cloak-and-dagger escapes, nor does it give undue stress to the sufferings and privations that are the normal lot of prisoners, especially prisoners of war. There are no accounts of sadistic brutalities. Rather, the central theme is the adaptability of the average GI to meet changing conditions, and to extract from such experiences, however grim, a measure of humor.

I cannot claim that the events depicted were typical. I can, and do, contend that they were factual, and it is my sincere belief that the following account presents, in true perspective, the saga of countless thousands of Allied prisoners who were fated to spend this chaotic period as unwilling guests of the Führer. Place names, dates, and characters are all factual.

Jack Dower, 1984

Foreword

In August 1984, my father, Jack Dower, set off on a journey to compose an epilogue to the book you are about to read. He was revisiting the place where he had been imprisoned forty years earlier. But, although he survived the Nazis, this time he did not make it home. In a profoundly sad irony, a massive heart attack took my father's life on the very German soil over which he had once triumphed.

Jack was born in Penryn, Cornwall, England, on May 3, 1919. His parents emigrated the following year and settled in Hartford, Connecticut, where Jack grew up an only child and graduated with honors from Hartford High School in 1935. Following the premature death of his father, Jack became the sole support for his mother, Ada, which deferred his military service until March 10, 1943, when he was inducted into the army and became a naturalized U.S. citizen. As a member of L Company, 179th Infantry, he saw combat first in North Africa, then at the Battle of Anzio, where he was captured by the Germans on February 18, 1944.

This book was many years in the making. From my childhood through my teens, I watched my father sit at our kitchen table, tapping away at his typewriter. It was all a mystery until his death, when I finally read what he had worked on for so long but seemed unlikely to see the light of day.

Thirty years later, I received a call from a history teacher in Louisville, Kentucky, who had mysteriously inherited a copy of Dad's manuscript. He was very enthusiastic about the book and offered to do everything he could to get this unique story into print. The dedication of that young man, Nathan Allen, and the marvels of modern technology made the idea of publishing this book possible.

Many others helped make the possible a reality: Brian Fitzpatrick, whose fine hand at editing maintained my dad's voice; my cousin Ken Dower, whose persistence in reaching out and connecting with Dad's fellow POWs confirmed the enduring emotional connection of this band of patriots; and my dad, whose determined spirit, I know, has guided this whole endeavor.

The process of preparing this book for publication has personally touched a few who were there in 1944–45, but mostly, the heroes of that time have moved on to greater things. God bless them all.

Susan Dower Carleson
June 2015

PART ONE

Captured

CHAPTER 1

Anzio

We huddled in the foxhole that crisp winter morning, February 18, 1944, two haggard-eyed infantrymen, unshaven and grimy, sweating out a blistering barrage that seemed as if every artillery piece in Christendom was trained on our muddy dugout. The shelling had gone on without letup for four hours. Spitfires intermittently roared overhead, peeling off one by one to loose their bombs at the cement canal bridge eighty feet to our left. The German was nondescript in his *Wehrmacht feldgrau* (armed forces field gray), a week's worth of gray stubble on chin and cheek, his eyes red rimmed with fatigue. I was even less prepossessing in my muddy olive drab, for I hadn't slept in fifty-four hours, and had spent the entire previous night crawling in mud and wading waist-deep in the maze of canals that crisscross the flat Anzio plain.

The damn canals had been our undoing. The previous night, dug in right on the front lines and virtually surrounded, Company L, 179th Infantry Regiment, 45th Infantry Division, had been ordered to pull back using the canals as cover. Somewhere in the inky blackness, twenty of us had taken a wrong turn and blundered two miles behind enemy lines. Single file, belt buckle–deep in icy canal water, we walked smack into a scorching tank battle. The whining and clashing of gears and treads was all around us. On our flank, we saw the eerie burning whiteness of semimolten metal from gutted tanks. We doubled back, only to come to grief.

About 3:00 A.M., on the roadway by the main canal, we plainly heard hobnailed German troops marching and officers shouting commands. It was obvious to the greenest replacement that we were in trouble. In desperation we plodded along, single file in pitch blackness, hoping that the lieutenant and sergeant up at the column's head could lead us out of the mess we were in before the sun came up. Without cover of darkness we would stand out like clay pigeons. In muted whispers a decision was made up front, and we marched off into bisecting canals, rifles in one hand well out of the water, the other hand grasping the belt of the man ahead.

Well aware that we were way off course and far behind enemy lines, we maintained absolute silence. Apprehension increased as the sky lightened. In a matter of minutes the sun rose above the horizon, and we were exposed in all our vulnerability.

Then it happened. A German machine gun unleashed its fury near the head of the column, and we ducked beneath the all too familiar, vicious zing of flying lead. But as abruptly as it had begun, the firing ceased. German commands were barked out, and the ugly snouts of a half dozen machine guns poked over the canal banks on both sides. Enough automatic weapons were trained on us to riddle every man in seconds. We were fifteen feet below the level of our enemy, in three feet of water, between riprapped canal banks that were completely devoid of cover and sloped up at 45-degree angles. All we had for targets were a couple of exposed helmets. We couldn't have found a more indefensible position if we had tried. The lieutenant turned, held up his hand to caution us to stay put and hold our fire, and clambered up the rocky escarpment. In a second or two he was back, flanked by two German machine gunners, and he beckoned us to climb out onto the plain.

As soon as we reached dry ground, it was clear to us that the German officer who had ordered the warning burst and allowed us to surrender had been a humanitarian of the first water. We were right in the middle of a troop detachment just bristling with firepower. Ringed by Germans, we were prodded up to a hardtop road that bridged the canal some two hundred feet farther ahead. The German commander pointed to a spot by the side of the road, and in no uncertain fashion made it clear we were to pile our rifles and ammo on that spot, and look lively about it.

The German commander was quite young and plentifully supplied with gold teeth that glistened in the rays of the bright Italian sun. Under normal circumstances we might have enjoyed the bright, crisp February morning, but this unexpected turn of events had us all feeling like hapless pawns in some somber chess match. The officer spoke only one English sentence, quite possibly his limit. His words were envious rather than sardonic. In a heavy accent, he said, "For you the war is over."

During the few minutes while our arms were being stacked, I noted that the place had the familiar look of a scene revisited. With surprise, I realized we were in one of our old positions, on the main canal just short of the factory that had been the focal point of a bitter swirling stalemate the week before. There, only eighty feet away, was a foxhole that had been my pride and joy when I dug it ten days earlier. A full five feet deep, and narrow, it had a shelflike recess about a foot down for handy storage of my rifle and bandoliers of ammo. Along both canal banks were other Company L holes, all now empty, as the massive German onslaught of the past three days had pushed the tiny Anzio perimeter three miles closer to the sea.

The Germans eyed us curiously. When I returned the scrutiny, I saw their rifles come up to the ready position. Reflex action, no doubt, but it behooved us all to inspect the toes of our shoes, at least for a while, when we saw how jumpy our captors were.

Our boys displayed a variety of emotions. Many were grim, others bewildered, as though unable to comprehend the fate that had befallen us. Quite a few looked and acted as though they had just won first prize in the Irish Sweepstakes. I must confess that I was in this latter category. Those of us who had been around on the front lines long enough to call ourselves veterans—and at Anzio three weeks was more than long enough—had been cognizant of the gravity of our situation most of the night and were almost resigned to death, or at best severe wounds. Everything in life, they say, is relative. Being taken prisoner was so infinitely preferable to either of the other possible outcomes that some of the boys were actually weeping for joy.

At this point the full import of what had occurred had not really registered with us. Although I suppose we all knew there would be grim days ahead, the fact that we had received a reprieve from probable death acted like a tonic. Life is dear, each precious minute of it, and we savored every invigorating breath by the canal bank. In the infantry you live for today, and you don't cross tomorrow's bridges until you come to them.

Just as we were being herded into line to march to the rear, all hell broke loose. Shells started coming our way, big ones. Neither the Germans nor we needed to be told what to do. All made beelines for the nearest hole. By chance I hopped into my foxhole of the previous week, and my German comrade tumbled in on my back. I blessed the day that I had fashioned such an admirable shelter. Being on the sharply angled canal bank on the side from which the shells were coming, and five feet below surface level to boot, we were in the best possible position to survive the barrage. Situated as we were there could be no direct hit on our hole, but we were vulnerable to airbursts or a hit on the diagonally opposed canal bank. Neither of these possibilities occurred, but for several hours we were bounced about like corks by the shells and bombs that exploded near us. Several shells landed up on the flat within thirty feet of our hole, sending shrapnel whizzing overhead and cascades of dirt raining on us. The concussion waves from each detonation sent us a good six inches off the ground. Fortunately, the Spitfires carried only a few relatively light antipersonnel bombs each, and they only made a few passes.

Every so often my German companion peered at me, and I could see a continuous twitching of his facial muscles and the cords in his throat. Fumbling in my tunic pocket for a cigarette, I saw his eyes blaze and the rifle come up. I stopped dead and motioned to my mouth, going through a pantomime of lighting and puffing a cigarette. He nodded assent, still

keeping his rifle poised. As I brought out the K ration cardboard folder of four Fleetwoods and proffered one, he grunted
and indicated that I was to light them both. In his state of obvious agitation, I doubted he could have managed to light the
match. Puffing away, eyes dilated and wincing at every shell
whistle, it was clear just how keyed up he was. I was eager for
the barrage to let up so I might be taken in tow by a more stable and calm guard.

I don't mean to imply that I was at ease, but to me, war
brought a certain amount of fatalism. You were in the hole.
There were no more preventive measures you could employ:
either the shell came in and got you or it didn't. In all fairness,
I will admit that never before had I been subjected to a barrage
of such fury, intensity, and length. German artillery, for all its
accuracy, had never been as unrelenting as this Allied bombardment. If the Jerries got many doses like this, who could
blame them for having a bad case of the jitters?

About two o'clock the firing ceased, and after a ten-minute
interval, just to make sure, commands were bellowed and my
foxhole mate motioned me to climb out. Just before we left the
foxhole, he held out his hand and spoke the German equivalent of good luck. After the handclasp I handed him the two
cigarettes that remained in the little cardboard box. A sort of
camaraderie existed among front-line troops, even among enemies, that was conspicuously lacking in rear echelon units.

German and GI heads alike started popping up out of the
ground, and with a minimum of delay our line of twenty prisoners was formed up on the road. A German jeep was up
ahead, two guards flanked the column, and another pair
brought up the rear. We set off at a brisk pace, heading away
from the front. The barrage had really unnerved our guards
and they hustled us along with frequent backward glances. It
was quite obvious that their spirits perked up with each rear-
ward step. So did ours.

When we had been on the road about an hour, a lone Spit-
fire came over and zoomed on the column for a strafing run.
We all hit the dirt in the roadside ditches as he dived. Making

his pass, he apparently miscalculated and overshot, for though several rounds came close, nobody was hit. Many of our boys thought that as he came on target he saw the color of our uniforms and purposely deflected his fire, but I have never subscribed to this theory. At the rate he was traveling he couldn't possibly differentiate between the uniforms. I ascribed our good fortune to poor marksmanship. We lay in the ditch until it was clear he was not coming back for another go.

The sun, settling lower in the sky at our backs, cast lengthening shadows as we left the flat Anzio plain and moved inland to some more rolling terrain. We passed some small farms, but saw no Italian civilians. We began passing the German rear echelon, ordnance depots, ammo dumps, field kitchens, and administrative facilities needed to back up the actual combat forces. To the uninitiated, it is always amazing to discover how many men are needed behind the lines to support one man up within small-arms range.

On two occasions we took ten-minute breaks, and we put the time to good use by filling our canteens. At one of these stops a GI next to me mentioned that he had heard two of the guards conversing in Polish. A few minutes later he started a soft-voiced conversation with the guard. The guard was cautious and not very communicative, but primed with a couple of cigarettes, he did give us some information. He said that a good part of his outfit were Poles, Czechs, and Austrians; they had arrived recently in Italy, having been diverted from Yugoslavia and Albania as soon as the Allied Anzio landing took place. As far as our immediate future was concerned, he knew only that the present guard detail was taking us just a few more miles to a town where we would be handed over to regular prison guards. This guard was on the flank, only about ten feet away from our column, so the talk was not overheard by any of the others.

About seven o'clock a German soldier on a bicycle overtook our group, and after a brief talk with the noncom in charge, gestured to a cluster of farm buildings up ahead a quarter of a mile. As we approached the buildings, the guards, by some shouting and more pointing, indicated that we would lie over here for the night. We had covered, I would guess, some twelve miles. Swinging into the cobbled stable yard, I glanced back into the setting sun at the front, where only sullen intermittent artillery rumbled.

The place was an unpretentious cobbled quadrangle steeped in farm smells, comprising a good-sized barn and one or two potting sheds or outbuildings a little way detached from the farmhouse proper. The Italian farmers had either sensibly taken off for the hills or, if they were on the premises, stayed in the main house, for we saw no one other than our guards that night. By this time it was getting dusky and a guard came from the main house with two oil lamps. We filed into a small building that housed some barrows, an assortment of small tools, rakes, and shovels, and a decrepit tractor. Four boys were led outside by a guard, returning in a few minutes with a load of straw, which we strewed on the earthen floor. Then came our introduction to the counting ritual. Led outside and lined up, we heard what was to become a familiar refrain: "*Ein, zwei, drei,*" etc. The Germans were absolute fanatics for counting, always out loud in bellows audible in the next township.

After we went back inside, one guard took up his station in a chair by the door. With unmistakable gestures he indicated that he was going to be awake all night and anyone getting too close to the door would sport a hole in his midriff the size of the Holland Tunnel. With this colorful admonition, he took the lamp and we stretched out on the straw.

Many of the boys took their shoes off that night, a luxury most of us hadn't indulged in for a month. I didn't, and was glad about it in the morning, for some of the lads had the devil's own time getting their shoes back on. Although sleep was days overdue, I didn't go to sleep for a while that night. The day's events had been so bewildering, and my future was so utterly unpredictable, that I lay awake about three-quarters of an hour before I finally conked off. My mates apparently were not as perturbed as I. Ten minutes after the guard took up his station by the door, the barn echoed to the snores and rasps of exhausted soldiers in all pitches and discords.

I awoke when something hard prodded my chest. Looking up, I saw it was a rifle butt. Others of our group were climbing to their feet, yawning and kneading their knuckles into their eyes. The sun was just coming up as we tumbled out into the stable yard to be lined up and counted again. The counting over, we went to a pump and splashed some frigid water over our faces and hands. This got the red corpuscles to chasing the white ones, and but for the feeling that some food would not be amiss, we were ready for the road again.

Once we got back to the road, we were handed over to a new group of guards. The Germans had dispensed with the jeep during the night, and we were now all on foot, guards and captors alike. Two guards headed the line of march and two others brought up the rear. We set off at a good pace, still to the east, climbing toward a town way off in the distance atop a sharp ridge.

Twice our little band received additional prisoners. The first time four Englishmen joined us, and the second time it was five GIs, one with his forearm bandaged and one with a thigh wound. The lad with the injured leg couldn't keep the pace, and shortly after joining the column he was put in a jeep as it passed us en route to the town.

There was quite a bit of traffic on the road, all military of course, and we were amazed to see how much the Germans used horses. Apparently the business end of the *Wehrmacht*, the panzer divisions, was mechanized to the hilt, but behind their "Sunday Punch," the rear echelons, field kitchens, ammo and fuel oil convoys, and so forth, were moved by horse-drawn wagon.

The road we traversed was the main street of the town we were approaching, and now for the first time we had a look at the Italian civilian populace this side of the line. There weren't very many about, just a few women scurrying along the road with the inevitable yard-long loaf of bread tucked under one arm, and some children playing in the alleys between the buildings. The women averted their eyes, pretending we didn't exist, but the children looked us over in the wide-eyed manner of children the world over.

By this time we were all damned hungry. When we were captured, most of us had a ration box with us, but the few crackers and can of cheese that these contained had been wolfed down during a break in the marching the previous afternoon.

With the bulk of the town behind us, we came upon a group of large buildings set well back from the main road, incongruous by virtue of their newness. We headed up a drive flanked by gardens to the main building. The structure was six stories high, of cement construction, with the severe, unadorned angular look of some block of ultramodern flats. Once inside, we realized that in peacetime this had been a large hospital. Now the corridors and wards had no furnishings or equipment of any type. Our footsteps echoed hollowly on the tiled flooring. We were led up to the fourth floor and put in what had once been an operating theater. Some of our boys were of Italian parentage, and from a few notices tacked to a bulletin board they gleaned that the place had specialized in children's diseases, particularly polio.

There was some indecision among the Germans as to the next step. We had sat around for a couple of hours when a guard brought in four loaves of bread, which we immediately divided and devoured. One of our new guards, a red-faced chap who had spent some time in the States, announced that we would spend the night at the hospital and be taken by truck the following morning to a regular prison camp on the outskirts of Rome.

Now, for the first time since our capture I guess, we all gave some serious thought to what the future might hold in store for us. Most of us agreed that we would ultimately be transported into Germany itself and put to work. None of us were so naive as to think that being a prisoner was going to be any picnic.

This respite also gave us a chance to talk to our British fellow prisoners, and we found that they had been taken four days before joining our little column. They had been captured about three miles from our position and taken to a German field hospital because several of their party had been severely wounded. These four had been sent, with one guard, to join us when it became known that a group of prisoners was in transit to the camp.

About this time I realized I had only three or four cigarettes left. Generally I carried a couple of packs as well as several of the K ration packs of four. The last couple days had made such inroads into my supply that I was about out. I didn't know it then, but I was about to break the habit for a long spell.

We were now far enough removed from the front that there was no combat noise other than an occasional rumbling of heavy artillery pieces. The only feature to remind us of the carnage was the constant dull red glow in the western sky. From our vantage point at the hospital windows, this light flickered in intensity in the manner of heat lightning back home. The frigid tiled floor did not make the best bed in the world, but we had to concede it was an improvement over the mud holes we had slept in over the past month.

Anzio had been truly miserable with regard to mud. The water table over the whole area had been only about eighteen inches below the surface. To be worth a damn, a foxhole, or even a slit trench, had to be at least twenty-four inches deep, so we had in effect done our sleeping in mud bathtubs, the water insidiously seeping into our burrows. The mornings were especially grim, as we would wake to find ourselves covered by sodden blankets and a skim of ice.

This night at the hospital we all got off to sleep in short order soon after it became dark. This was a habit we were to pick up more and more during our sojourn in Italy as prisoners. When it got dark, with no lights, there wasn't much point in staying awake, and further, we found that sleep was the best way to alleviate our constant hunger, which became more and more acute as time went on.

Morning came with no sign of our captors except for two guards down in the courtyard, four stories below, leaning against the wall and enjoying an early morning smoke. At ten o'clock two guards came up the stairs and brought us down to ground level for the usual counting, followed by the announcement that the trucks would arrive in an hour. The pale wintry sun was no match for the chill winds that swept down from the Apennines.

Two trucks rolled up soon after, and divided into two groups of about fifteen, we climbed over the tailgates. One guard rode up front with the driver in each truck, and a jeep followed the little convoy. The jeep carried two guards, in addition to the driver, each with automatic weapons. Our course led over a succession of ridges to the east.

After twenty miles we approached the outskirts of a large city. The contour of the land flattened out, and the towns were more closely spaced. We started passing good-sized factories, and several times went over multiple-track railroad crossings. As the perimeter of Rome came closer, the ground was covered with a light blanket of snow with the grimy look of having lain there several days. With a lurch and shift of gears, the truck swung off to the left and up a slight grade, bringing us to a massive barbed-wire gate. We were hustled out of the trucks, formed into a slouchy column of twos, and marched into the first of what was to prove a long series of prison camps: Ferra Sabrina.

CHAPTER 2

Transit Camps

Ferra Sabrina consisted of about twenty cement one-story shedlike buildings, with one larger building adjacent to the entrance gate. Barbed-wire fencing about eighteen feet high girdled the square encampment, and each of the four corners had an enclosed platform atop spindly legs. Their function was obvious even to prison camp novices.

In front of the large building—which proved to be the mess kitchen, guards' quarters, and administrative offices—was an immense iron pot. As a long line of GIs and Tommies filed past, each man was given a dipper of soup. Our coming did not evoke any great stir of interest from either the guards or the motley crew of prisoners that had preceded us. The prisoners all glanced our way, and some waved, but there were no shouts or greetings, and every man zealously guarded his place in line. The British were easily distinguished from the GIs with their berets, leather jerkins, and buckled-at-the-ankle battle-dresses, which resembled grossly exaggerated plus fours.

After we were lined up and counted once more, our guards pointed to the dwindling mess line and indicated we should hurry if we wanted any chow. Some prisoners who had finished their meal offered us the use of their cups and tin cans as we all made a beeline for the soup kettle. We were just in time, as there wasn't much left in the pot. We each received a dipperful of cloudy-looking soup. Its greatest virtue was that it was hot. As far as quantity, it came to about a cupful, and from the taste the basic ingredients were about twenty gallons of water per dozen potatoes. Just the same, it went down well.

Our meal over, a British sergeant came up and led us into a hut, where we were each issued a thin blanket and a soup container. The sergeant told us to find the best sleeping quarters we could. There was little to choose from among the huts, which were all doorless, windowless, and equally crowded.

Of the twenty men from L Company taken in the canal that morning, there was only one man I knew well. The others were acquaintances of a few days, or weeks at most, as our outfit had incurred its full measure of casualties, and fresh replacements made up the bulk of each company. There was one lad though, Johnny DiCrecchio of Portland, Maine, who had been with me since my first month in the army. We met on the troop train going from Camp Devens, Massachusetts, where New Englanders were inducted into the army, down to Camp Croft in Spartanburg, South Carolina, for basic training. We had shared the same barracks at Croft, then on to Camp Chenango, Camp Shanks, and the troop carrier *Santa Paula* to Algiers in an eighteen-day convoy. We crossed North Africa to Bizerte together, and then we both joined L Company on the same day when they were just off the Salerno beaches. By sheer chance, we were assigned to the same squad and consequently gazed down identical German gun barrels when we were captured that fateful February 18.

To anyone versed in army methods of constantly shuffling personnel, transfers, replacements, and the like, the coincidence was almost unbelievable, but it worked out that way, and I was to be with Johnny every day for the next year and three months. By the end of the war I felt a relationship to Johnny akin to that of a real brother.

Johnny and I took our blankets, staked out fifteen feet of floor space in one of the huts, and hit the hay. It was twilight when we entered the hut, and with no illumination of any kind we could barely see the man sleeping next to us.

In the cold gray dawn that followed, we were up and about to explore our new surroundings, and what we found did not inspire enthusiasm. A flat, hard-packed clay rectangle was lined with gray cement sheds. The group of buildings was enclosed by a sinister barbed-wire fence standing out against a bleak February sky. The guard complement numbered about thirty Germans, and they were just as slovenly and grubby looking as the camp itself.

Ferra Sabrina, as we had surmised, was on the outskirts of Rome. It had once been a garrison for Italian troops, but for the past two years had been operated solely as a prison camp. The camp was not nearly as large as those we were to encounter later. I would guess that it could house, at a maximum, 1,000 prisoners, and at the moment it had seemingly achieved capacity. We were told that it was used only as a transit camp and that every week or so batches of prisoners were shipped out to northern Italy and ultimately Germany.

There had been no prisoner shipments for the past four weeks, reportedly because Allied air strikes had repeatedly plastered the relatively few rail lines to the north. This news came from a downed RAF flyer who contended that the mountainous terrain required hundreds of viaducts and railroad bridges, which had been getting a thorough working over by the Desert Air Force. One severely damaged viaduct could immobilize many miles of track.

A cupful of watery soup was the only item on the bill of fare at Ferra Sabrina, and only one meal per day was served with any degree of regularity, in the late afternoon. The boys who preceded us said that once in a while a bonus ration was doled out in the morning, but that this was an infrequent occurrence and we shouldn't bank on it.

Wandering from hut to hut, we met and chatted with a cosmopolitan array of fighting men: Scots, Gurkhas, Aussies, Canadians, New Zealanders, South Africans, and a few Cypriots, as well as the familiar GIs and Tommies. A great many of these had been longtime prisoners of the Italians, but had been released when Italy capitulated on September 3, 1943. After dodging about in the hills in a vain endeavor to rejoin Allied forces, most had been picked up again by the Germans or by bands of Italian Fascists. These boys had fascinating stories to tell about their three or four weeks on the loose. Though none

of them had any great love for the Germans, they were unanimous in claiming that the treatment we were now accorded was
infinitely preferable to that doled out by the Italians. Here, for
the first time, we were to hear of that mysterious and elusive
item, the Red Cross parcel.

The reactions of Italian prison guard detachments to the
September 3 surrender had been many and varied. Lots of
prisoners were wished good luck and marched out of the gates.
Other camps were staffed by diehard Fascists who remained
loyal to Mussolini. These camps held the prisoners at gunpoint
while hastily summoning German troops to the scene. Of the
great numbers of prisoners who were temporarily freed, a relative few had elected to try to make their way to Switzerland and
internment. Most had chosen to make for the south, hoping to
hook up with the British and American troops then beating
their way north from Calabria.

As it turned out, those who made for Switzerland had far
better luck. The Italian partisans were strongest in the north-
ernmost provinces and had quite an efficient organization to
aid and abet escapees. The prisoners were sheltered and passed
from village to village in cross-country night journeys. They
were ultimately led in small groups over the passes into Switzerland. Rumor had it that the Italian guides of such parties were
paid off at a fixed-rate COD per prisoner.

Quite a number of the prisoners at Ferra Sabrina had
worked their way south, only to find the German lines impene-
trable. Others were informed on by Italian civilians while en
route to the front. Several of these men had wandered about
for months in a vain search for freedom, and according to
them, there were many others still eluding recapture.

A few had gone as close as they dared to the actual combat
lines, then tried to make an end run in small fishing boats. It
was feared that these, for the most part, had been lost at sea.
Two had made it as far as five miles north of the Montecassino
abbey, holing up in a cave in anticipation that the Allies would
sweep past their hideout in a matter of days. It must have been
bitterly frustrating for them to see the Montecassino area

become a bloody stalemate. After six weeks of subsisting on acorns, berries, and the like, they emerged from their grotto to surrender to a roving German patrol.

A group of three Limeys had an even more fantastic tale. They had made for the Ancona–Pescara sector, worked their way through German lines posing as civilian farmhands, and were within a few hundred yards of a British command post when they were picked up by a reconnoitering British patrol. The patrol leader was mistrustful of the civilian clothing, despite their explanations, and refused to allow them to go the short distance to British HQ, where the authenticity of their stories could be checked. He insisted they remain with the patrol, which had just a bit farther to go before completing the mission and returning. As luck would have it, the patrol was ambushed within a few minutes, and all their efforts went up in smoke.

About noontime a German guard came through the huts, shouting that all of the new prisoners who had arrived on the previous day were to line up in front of the commandant's office. Entering one by one, we were given cards to fill out for Red Cross records, listing our name, serial number, rank, hometown address, next of kin, and other pertinent data. The two uniformed clerks who took down this information spoke perfect English complete with British inflection. We were told that the recorded information would be forwarded to Geneva and would be used to notify our parents or wives of our status as POWs. The whole proceeding only took about an hour, after which we rejoined the rest of the boys and whiled away the time until supper.

We never were given any formal interrogation, and we later found that this was normal procedure except for officers of fairly high rank. Actually, this made quite a lot of sense. To be of value, any information had to be secured quickly after capture, in view of the extreme fluidity of the usual military situation. Also, there would be little the average army private or corporal could convey that the *Wehrmacht* did not already know.

We had all now acquired a tin can or cup and a spoon. This was the only cutlery needed for guests of the Third Reich in

1944. The tin cans had seemingly never been washed, and scaly deposits coated the inner surfaces. By this time we had long since lost all traces of being finicky about grub, and the fact that the crockery would never have been given the Good House-keeping Seal of Approval was a matter of small import.

By now the sensation of hunger was really acute. We thought and talked of little other than food. The prison camp veterans assured us that we would become inured to the hunger, and that under such conditions stomachs shrank to the point that a bare minimum of nourishment would suffice. This sounded like a pretty dubious theory to us newcomers, but we were to find out the hard way.

At the extreme opposite end of the camp from the admin-istration building was a hut from which came the most horrible stench imaginable. This was the camp latrine. Initially this toi-let facility was designed with brick footrests set in the concrete floor, about fifteen inches from each other. Set between and about twelve inches to the rear of the footrests was a hole about as big around as a plate. The idea of this primitive arrange-ment was that you put one foot on each brick and then aimed for the hole. Unfortunately, the last several thousand cus-tomers had been extremely poor marksmen, so now the entire floor area was considered a fair target. Johnny and I tried to keep to windward of this structure while at Ferra Sabrina, for though we certainly weren't fastidious, the stench from this building could be cut with a knife.

On a related topic, we were informed by the camp veterans that there were two distinct reactions to prison fare as far as bowel movements were concerned. Either you made a flying dash to the latrine every fifteen minutes, or you would go for a month or more without need of these facilities. The former set of circumstances was claimed to be highly dangerous, easily leading to dysentery and often death. Johnny and I were defi-nitely charter members of the Non-Latrine-Goers Guild, and for this we were sincerely thankful.

About 5:00 P.M. whistles were blown and the queue formed before the soup kettle. Johnny and I fell in line for our ration.

On a red-letter day, the cook somehow found a few turnips to add to the potato soup.

On the fourth day after our arrival, we were all lined up on the packed clay area immediately in front of the combined HQ and soup kitchen. Something big was in the offing. Three officers came out of the building with a sheaf of papers, and as names were called, those summoned formed into a group near the entrance gate. About 150 men were told they were being transferred to another camp that afternoon. Our names were not on the list, though we were rooting hard throughout the call, for we'd had a bellyful of Ferra Sabrina. To us, anything else couldn't help but be an improvement. There was no need for packing, and soon ten trucks rolled in the gate to be boarded by the departing group. Johnny and I were fated to be stuck at Ferra Sabrina for another ten days.

Some three days after the first group movement, as we were collecting our soup one afternoon, Johnny called to me, "Look at this, Jack!" In his cup was a horse's eyeball, apparently thrown in the soup for good measure. As we were examining it, one of the older inmates came over and piped up, "'Ere, mate, I'll take that if you don't want it," and to our amazement gulped it down with seeming relish. Johnny grinned at me and said, "I hope we never get quite that hungry, Jack."

A week after the first batch moved out, there was another truck convoy of prisoners, once again about 150 in the group. Three days later there was another call, and this time both Johnny and I grabbed the brass ring. My name was called early on the list, and for quite a while I was fearful that at last Johnny and I had come to our parting of the ways, but just a few names from the tail end of the list came the call "John DiCrecchio." The roster was made up just before soup time, and the assembled group was told to form ranks by the gate the next morning to board transport to another camp.

Johnny and I were jubilant that night. We had seen as much of Ferra Sabrina as we wanted to and were eager to be on the move again. We all had the fixation that the sooner we could get to permanent camps, the sooner we would get our hands on

the Red Cross parcels. We didn't sleep too well that night, and
at the first shrill of the whistle the next morning, we hustled up
to the loading area. I guess everyone in the chosen group felt
the same way, for there were no laggards.

As we stood huddled in the gray mistiness of early morning,
the sun came up a golden ball in the east. It was the first fine
day since our arrival, and we hoped it portended better things
to come.

Johnny and I made it into the second truck. As each man
climbed over the tailgate, he was given a slab of bread and a
square can of some kind of potted meat. The cans were of the
key-opening variety and the same shape and size as the familiar
corned beef can. A stir of excitement swept the group as we
were given our first solid food in four weeks.

There were seven trucks in the convoy, each loaded with
twenty men. A guard rode in the cab with the driver, and a jeep
followed the last truck. The guards in the jeep all had Spandau
machine guns, and those riding in the trucks had conventional
rifles.

The column got moving with a minimum of delay, and we
were soon rolling briskly through the most pleasant part of Italy
that we had seen to date. The sun shone brightly, but the wind
was cold. We climbed ridges, each steeper than the last, and
descended down hairpin turns as the trucks lurched into valleys
and crossed racing streams. The crests of the hills to the east
were powdered with snow, contrasting the somber green of the
cypress-clad lower slopes.

Many of the boys wolfed down the best part of the bread
and meat during the first few miles, but Johnny and I and some
of the others figured we would wait a while. There was no way
of estimating how long we would be on the road, and it was anybody's guess when rations would be issued again. Just the feel
of the bread and the tinned beef did wonders for our spirits.
We nibbled away at the slab of black bread but held out on the
beef until midafternoon. We had learned from other prisoners
that the Germans normally used rail transport for any prisoner
movements of great length, and as the morning wore on with

no sign of a transfer to trains, it strengthened our belief that we were not being moved very far, at least not out of Italy.

About three o'clock the lead truck pulled off to the side of the road. We were in a grove of oak through which coursed a brook. Though the guards were alert and weapons were in firing position, they seemed in good spirits and told us we had about fifteen minutes to stretch our legs and fill up on water if we chose. Right in the middle of this little glen, the brook widened to a pool where several drivers were filling pails for the truck radiators.

Johnny and I had a good swig of the icy spring water. As we filed back to the trucks for the second leg of our journey, we opened our cans of beef. To us, that beef tasted far better than any meal in memory. We savored each and every mouthful. By this time, relying more on the bird in the hand than the one in the bush, we prudently saved half of our meat ration for whatever lay ahead. On and on we rolled, the sun now shining from our left and the country more scenic with every passing mile.

The sun was low on the horizon when the first truck turned off the highway and onto a dirt road. The trucks bounced down the country lane in low gear, scraping past tree branches that whipped back only to be pushed aside by the next truck. Apparently we were nearing the end of our journey. Dusk set in after two or three miles of slow progress, and we were unloaded. Each truckload of prisoners walked in the glare of the following vehicle's headlights, the guards riding on the running boards with their weapons poised.

After fifteen minutes on foot we reached a high barbed-wire gate, complete with striped sentry box and railroad crossing–type wooden cross-arm roadblock. Once we entered the camp, there was the inevitable head count, and we were curtly told to go into any barracks for the night. In the gloom we could distinguish little as we filed along and entered an unoccupied barracks. One of the guards spoke fair English, and he gave us strict orders to stay inside that night, because the guards patrolling the camp perimeter and manning the searchlights and guns in the corner watchtowers had instructions to shoot at anything that moved after dark. A cursory inspection showed us that structurally, at any rate, our new quarters were far superior to Ferra Sabrina. These barracks had wooden floors, doors, and heavily shuttered windows, and were partitioned into rooms. Once inside, we wasted little time getting to sleep.

The next morning we awoke full of curiosity about our new surroundings. Stepping out into the yard area, we noted that the camp, slightly smaller than Ferra Sabrina, was nestled in a deep, cuplike valley. Steep wooded slopes rose all around us. On the crest of the high hill to our right was a town, and the early morning sun gleamed on the gilded dome of a church tower and the red-tiled roofs of the adjacent houses. Terraced vineyards held their precarious perch on the ground sloping down sharply behind the row of houses. Like so many towns, this one seemed nothing more than a concentration of attached buildings strung along the main highway for about a mile.

The prisoners who had arrived in the camp before us, mainly British, briefed us on our new home. Like us, they had not been there very long, no more than three weeks at the most. They told us the camp, La Torina, was a few miles south of Firenze, or Florence. La Torina was yet another transit camp. When we moved from here it would, in all probability, be to Austria or Germany itself.

At Ferra Sabrina there had been no officers among the prisoners, but here at La Torina there were several British officers, including a medical officer and a major. The major, by virtue of being the ranking officer, acted as commandant and spokesman for the prisoners in their contacts with our German captors.

While Ferra Sabrina had been grim, gray, and forbidding, La Torina was relatively new, with whitewashed stucco barracks in reasonably good repair. Until recently an Italian Army training detachment had been quartered here. The Limeys said the daily food ration was far more edible than the Ferra Sabrina slop, and in addition there were occasional issues of ersatz coffee.

The guards were a far cry from the unshaven lot who had been our keepers at Ferra Sabrina. That crew had been the dregs of the *Wehrmacht*, with a slovenly bearing and the animation of robots. The guard detail at La Torina was infinitely more soldierly in every way: clean-shaven, alert, their gear in good order. They were obviously well-disciplined garrison troops. At La Torina the German officers were on the ball and frequently in evidence on the parade grounds and around the administration building. They were not especially well disposed toward us and were fanatics on counting rituals, which were staged about three times a day, rain or shine.

By now we knew a few German words, mainly *schnell* (quick), *verflucht* (damn it), *los* (loose, set free), *achtung* (attention), *raus* (out, outside, get out), and the numbers up to twenty. We had also learned to differentiate the uniform stripes and pips and could determine who were *Feldwebels* (high-ranking sergeants), *Unteroffiziers* (lower ranking noncoms), and the one resplendent *Hauptmann* (captain). The chests of most of the guards bore the Iron Cross suspended by its red-white-and-black striped ribbon. Apparently it was a decoration handed out almost as promiscuously as our basic training Marksman award. The campaign ribbons had no significance to us, but we were intrigued by the red-and-white target-like circles on the peaks of their gray overseas caps.

A distinct difference between the two camps was the feeling of some measure of security afforded by the brisk way the Allied officers rightly assumed their obligations and took charge of our activities. We felt we had an advocate, or friend at court, though we all knew this was more psychological than actual, as the protests of our officers would not prove very effectual in any major matter. Nevertheless, it was comforting to know there was someone around who would go to bat for us if need be. Such occasions sometimes arose, and the German commandant invariably gave audience to the British officers and listened to the complaints and requests with attentiveness and courtesy. Most of these calls had to do with the need for adequate medical supplies. Once in a while the request would be complied with.

It was also reassuring to have a competent medical officer in the camp, though we all knew that his stock of supplies did not run much beyond aspirins, ointments, and bandages. Despite these shortcomings, he did his best to see that the health of the prisoners was maintained as well as could be expected under these trying conditions.

Johnny and I had now punched so many new notches in our belts that our pants hung off us like old sacks. Most of our barracks buddies talked incessantly of food, prattling off imaginary seven-course meals in the minutest detail. We wanted no part of such foolish chatter. Jesus Christ, it was bad enough to be constantly physically aware of the hunger pangs without having some damn fool rub it in with such idle talk.

La Torina was under exceptionally close security measures, with incessant countoffs. We were told that the heightened discipline stemmed from the escape of two Tommies three weeks before our arrival. The story went that seven Italian workmen had been engaged for several days laying a pipeline through a section of the camp. The Limeys had prevailed upon two of them to wear two sets of pants and shirts one day when coming on the job. During the morning, the extra garments had been secreted behind one of the camp barracks, to be donned by the escapees, who had strolled out of the main gate late in the afternoon carrying a length of large-diameter soil pipe. Their absence was not discovered until the following noontime.

After the escape, La Torina had become a disciplinary hellhole. In retaliation, the entire camp body was forced to stand at attention in the drill yard, often in pouring rain. Food rations were drastically cut, and the British officers were interrogated for hours on end. The guards paid furious attention to detail to atone for their unfortunate lapse. The camp's routine was only now beginning to return to normal, fully three weeks after the incident.

The barracks at La Torina were bisected by a central corridor running the entire length of the building. There were three good-sized rooms on each side of this central passageway. Bedded in twelve to a room, we had ample floor space and elbow room. Each barracks had a cold water tap and a wooden tub for morning washups.

Things were systematized at La Torina, a welcome departure from Ferra Sabrina, where everything had been on a catch-as-catch-can basis. This was essentially due to the British officers, who saw to it that equity prevailed. Each room had its rationer, or "food divider," a chore I performed for my room. It was considered a tribute to enjoy such great esteem from your fellow prisoners that they permitted you to divide and distribute the meager rations. At two o'clock a whistle would blow and the dividers would all go to the ration hut for the issue for their room. One day it would be the staple soup, but on alternate days there was an issue of solid food. This would be a six-inch cube of bread, a cube of margarine, and some sort of cheese paste or spread. The bread was not the white fluffy variety, but a heavy black rye. This was brought back to our respective rooms to be cut into twelve equal portions and distributed. Courtesy demanded that the "divider" take the last portion so there could be no charge of unfairness. The boys jokingly called me "Old Micrometer Eye Power" and swore that I cut the bread and margarine as though I were splitting the Kohinoor diamond.

Other than the counting formations and the regulation that we were all in barracks and the door locked come nightfall, we had no duties or assignments. We spent our days conversing with our fellow prisoners and strolling about the camp grounds, keeping to the windward side of the latrine and well away from the inner perimeter of barbed wire surrounding the camp.

After the first few days, most of the boys found they were providing living quarters for hungry tribes of lice, and on fairly warm days the boys spent most of their time inspecting the seams of their underclothes and shirts for the unwelcome visitors, cracking them expertly between their thumbnails as they captured them. For some reason or another, Johnny and I and a few others did not encounter this problem. Perhaps we were so grimy that even the lice scorned us. In several cases the problem was acute, with lice colonies staking out claims in the prisoners' eyebrows. One British lad had so many that after several nights of absolutely no sleep he just went berserk, clawing off all clothing and scratching himself into a mass of bleeding furrows. He was taken to the camp hospital by his buddies, a mental case, at least temporarily.

The weather at La Torina became progressively warmer, and the early Italian spring sun made a pretty sight glimmering on the tiled roofs of the town so high above us. Within a couple of weeks, we had lived in such proximity with our British buddies that we had become familiar with their various dialects: Cockney, Lancashire, and Scottish. The use of many of their expressions had become almost second nature. Such expressions as "Jerry," "Eyetie," "Padre," and "M.O." became part of our normal speech, and the adjective "bloody" larded our conversations.

About three weeks after we arrived, the camp commandant announced on the parade ground that we would all be moving out the following day, except for those who were hospitalized. This was momentous news indeed. Opinion was evenly divided as to whether this was the long haul to Germany or whether we were going to another Italian transit camp.

CHAPTER 3

Through the Brenner Pass by Boxcar

Early in the morning we formed ranks for our final head count at La Torina. In a column of fours—led, flanked, and followed by a full complement of German guards—we hiked out the main gate and walked about three miles along a pleasant secondary road through farming country.

On a railroad spur stood a string of twelve Italian boxcars. No engine was in sight. We were shepherded in, thirty-three to a boxcar. I should point out that these were narrow-gauge European boxcars, less than half the size of a U.S. railroad car. Each of us had barely enough room to take a deep breath.

Just before entering the cars, we were each given a whole half loaf of bread and a chunk of *wurst*, or sausage. Inside the car, right in the middle, was a nail keg, the German version of sanitary plumbing. A skimpy layer of straw covered the floor of the car. This much we saw before the door slammed shut and we were in pitch blackness.

Feet milled about on the cinder roadbed outside and commands were bawled out continuously. After an hour a crash and lurching of the car threw us all in a heap, informing us that the engine had been coupled. Soon we were underway.

As the train rolled onward, we became better adjusted to the dark and could move about a bit. Every few hours the train would halt with a shudder and squeal of brakes. We would stay motionless for an hour or so, and then start up again. As a prison train we presumably had little priority on the rails and were frequently shunted off on sidings to make way for more important cargo.

There was one small chink in the sidewall at the far end of the car, and we lined up to take turns squinting through it and getting a breath of fresh air. After our second trip to the little gap, Johnny and I decided it wasn't worth the effort. The crack was so small you couldn't see anything, and the return trip back to our reserved floor space, after spending two minutes at the crack, brought forth curses from our prostrate fellow travelers as our boots landed inevitably on feet and skulls. There was a minute difference in light as night fell, and most of us, by now able to sleep on a picket fence, conked off. The chunk of bread and piece of sausage, wrapped up in a bit of cloth, made our pillow.

Our slumbers were frequently disturbed when we were stepped on by boys making their way to and from the nail keg toilet. The keg soon became filled to overflowing, to the extreme discomfort of those sleeping close to it. During the early hours of the morning, as the train rounded a curve, the keg and its user toppled over, bathing the floor of the car in excrement. Loud were the curses of the travelers who were inundated. Johnny and I were thankful that we had been among the first to enter the car and had staked out our claims well toward the corner. The next morning the stench in our compartment would have stifled any normal person. Undaunted, we pulled out our bread and sausage and ate about a third of the ration. Prison life had certainly dulled our sensibilities.

The second day and night passed much like the first. We seemed to be rolling about half the time and parked on some siding the rest of the time. About noon on the second day, while on a siding, we heard footsteps outside and the door was rolled back, blinding us with brilliant sunlight. Three guards supervised as two of our boys emptied our nail keg privy in the brush alongside the tracks. After returning the keg, these same prisoners were led away again, and then came back with a washtub full of water and four tin cups. The tub was set on the car floor by the door, and under the watchful eyes of the guards we had our fill of water. All told, the car door was open for about fifteen minutes. Looking out, we could see we were in a country of dark high hills, almost big enough to be called mountains.

The door slammed shut, and in ten minutes we were on our way again. We valued the halt for the sunshine, water, and fresh air. The toilet emptying was quite farcical, for in a few miles the interior of the car was as ripe as ever.

As we had no way of computing the miles traveled, we could only vaguely guess at our location. To those of us who had some knowledge of Italian geography, we could only be northbound, which either meant going through the Brenner Pass into Austria or else swinging northwest past Turin and into southern France. This latter possibility seemed so unlikely that we were all reasonably sure that we were Austria bound.

About three hours after the water stop we lurched to a halt again. The outside sounds were much different. The whistles and hiss of steam from other engines and the clatter of cars passing over switch points indicated we were in a railhead of some size. The door was opened again, and level with the floor of our car was the cement platform of a railroad station. On the platform just outside were two women, probably German by their blonde coloring, in Red Cross aprons and caps, tending a large soup kettle. Under the watchful eyes and rifles of the guards, we were each given a dipperful of a delicious hot broth. I remember clearly that there were lots of rice, peas, and celery in the soup, but most of all I recall the pleasant smile of the Red Cross worker, the first compassionate glance in months. The soup had a wonderful effect, making us all feel 1,000 percent better. Even the sick—and we had many of them—brightened up as they were helped along the platform.

Gazing down the platform in the dusk of early evening, I made out the name BOLZANO on the station sign and saw doors in the station labeled CUSTOMS and BORDER CHECKPOINT. We were at the southern, Italian end of the famed Brenner Pass. Next stop, Austria.

After the soup, the train was shunted over onto another set of tracks and was motionless for the rest of the night. In the

morning we were off again, and soon had another short stop
for water. The sun was shining, and snowclad mountain peaks
reared up in magnificent splendor before an azure sky. Against
a backdrop of precipitous cliffs, we could see the sign above
the station ahead: INNSBRUCK. We were now on Austrian soil, at
the prewar international mecca of winter sports.

The soup the evening before had stood us in good stead, so
Johnny and I waited until the early afternoon to polish off the
scant remains of our bread and *wurst.* By nightfall of the third
day many of the boys could no longer stand, and the dysentery
was the worst I had ever seen. It was ominously clear that unless
we got where we were going, and got there damn fast, a lot of
boys would have to be carried out of the boxcar, and we'd be
lucky if we didn't have any corpses.

Close to noon on the fourth day the train shuddered to a
halt. Somehow this stop had an air of finality about it. Doors
were flung open along the entire length of the train, and everybody was ordered outside. Those of us who could stand
needed no urging. Scrambling out of the stinking black car, we
hastily formed ranks on the trap rock of the roadbed. The
strong ones supported the weak ones, and the two or three
who were in really bad shape were carried in stretchers to a
waiting German army truck.

Eyes blinking in the unaccustomed bright light, we looked
about in wonder. There were three large houses in a row
fronting a road that paralleled the tracks across a short field.
They were a far cry from the Italian houses we had seen these
past six months. The large two-story buildings were somewhat
boxlike in appearance but looked immaculate, with well-kept
gardens front and rear. They were of cement construction, one
lemon yellow, the other two beige, all with gabled roofs and
half-timbered upper floors. We had arrived in Germany.

CHAPTER 4

Stalag VII A, Moosburg

We didn't have to wonder where the camp was. Set back only a half mile from the tracks, we could see an enormous installation bristling with barbed wire, machine guns, and searchlight towers. The column trudged through the massive gates and halted before a small cement building. We were told to sit down and that we would be called in individually to be registered.

As we broke ranks and sat down on the hard-packed sand, a group of GI and British noncoms came up, gave each man a couple of cigarettes, and said that in a short while we would be given permanent quarters and Red Cross food parcels. This was just too much good news at one time. In our weakened condition, most of us sobbed and wept like children.

Soon it was our turn to be registered. In a neat room lined with filing cabinets were four German clerks behind desks. They asked our names, serial numbers, next of kin, etc., all of which they typed on official index cards. We were individually photographed and told that the pictures, when developed, would be affixed to our case history cards. In another room, metal plates were stamped with our *Gefangenenummer*, or prisoner number. These were like GI dog tags, only slightly larger in size. Cords were furnished to fasten these identity discs around our necks. All this was done in an atmosphere of quiet efficiency. The interviewers spoke excellent English, and in extracting the needed information seemed very pleasant, assuring us that the data collected would be forwarded to Geneva in a few days and that our parents should be conversant with our status and general whereabouts in a month or less. Leaving this place through a rear door, we waited until about eighty of us were assembled, then followed our guards a few hundred feet to another long shedlike structure.

We entered a large anteroom filled with rows of wicker-wire baskets of the type used in swimming pool locker rooms, row after row on racks that went up to the ceiling. We stripped, put our clothing in a basket, and retained one of the numbered basket tags. We were in for a long-overdue bath! As we filed through a doorway, small bars of soap were given to every third man, and we found ourselves in an enormous steam-filled shower room. How we luxuriated under the scalding water and billowing soap suds. The guards gave us twenty minutes under the showers while our clothing was being deloused. The baskets of clothing were baked in ovens at terrific temperatures, and we could be sure that not even the hardiest louse would survive that treatment.

I enjoyed that shower as I have never enjoyed anything else, before or since. It was just wonderful. We actually felt human again.

Leaving the shower room, we filed into a third room where we dried off, then passed on to still another room. At regular intervals I heard roars of laughter, but couldn't fathom what was going on until it was my turn. Sitting on a three-legged stool was an old Russian soldier. He must have been sixty-five, with gray whiskers, a pot, and a paintbrush. As I moved abreast of him, he dipped the brush into a can of watery fluid and applied it liberally to those parts where lice would most likely seek refuge. For a second there was a sensation of coolness, then it seemed as if my genitals were on fire. With a yelp I leaped for the ceiling. After a few seconds the fire passed away and I could stand around watching the next victim do his best to shatter the standing high jump record. I never found out the ingredients of that brew, but I can guarantee its effectiveness. The stuff was so potent it's a wonder anything remained of the entire painted area. Just imagine splashing muriatic acid on your crown jewels.

Leaving the "paint room," we were given our baskets of thoroughly deloused clothing, and donning them, we felt like new men. Outside we were turned over in groups to British noncoms who led us to our barracks.

Our hut commander was a South African, and on the way to the barracks he did his best to answer our hundreds of questions. We were now at *Stalag* (*Stammlager*, or base camp) VII A, at Moosburg, Bavaria, relatively close to Munich. The camp housed thousands of prisoners of all nationalities, most of these groups set off in separate barbed wire–enclosed compounds of their own. The British, American, and Commonwealth troops were all in one massive compound.

Red Cross parcels were issued weekly. The issue was normally a half parcel per man per week, but a recent increase in supplies received had made it possible to issue a full parcel weekly to each individual. Issuing day had been two days before we arrived, but the new boys would all be given parcels at the barracks later that afternoon or evening.

As we walked along, savoring our first cigarettes in weeks, we stared at rows of hundreds of prison huts in the separate Yugoslav, Russian, and French compounds. Our leader told us there were at least 12,000 prisoners in this enormous camp, and at least 4,000 of these were British or Americans. We turned off the roadway to a barracks identical in all respects to the dozens that flanked it on either side. This would be our home at *Stalag* VII A.

Our barracks was the typical German prison camp design with which we were to become intimately familiar: a one-story cement rectangle with center entrance, center exit, and one central aisle along the long axis linking the two doors. The buildings, all from the same floor plan, were about forty-five feet by eighty feet inside. Three-tiered bunks ran at right angles to the outer walls from the center aisle. The bunks were composed of rough two-by-four uprights with six-inch-high boxlike arrangements for sleeping. Each bunk was butted end to end with two more bunks, and each set of three bunks butted side by side with another set of three bunks. Side aisles ran between each set of six connected bunks, making each group a little island sleeping eighteen men.

The bottoms of the bed boxes were a few wooden slats. As we entered, we were issued thin palliasses of straw to place on the slats. These were always called "Pollyasses" in prison lingo.

At the far end of the barracks was an open space beyond the last rows of bunks, where a few wooden tables and benches stood. Against the wall was a large oven, but only infrequently was there a coal issue that permitted it to be lit.

In each barracks there was one small detached room just inside the front door. This was probably the sleeping quarters of the German noncom in charge when the camp was used in its normal function, as a troop barracks. In prison camps, these rooms were used by the hut commanders, in our case the South African noncom, and boasted a cot, a chair, and a crude desk.

Half an hour after entering the barracks and being assigned bunks, we were instructed to line up outside the hut commander's room for a Red Cross issuance. Excitement was at fever pitch. We were told that instead of the usual individual Red Cross parcels, we would be sharing New Zealand Bulk Rations, which would tide us over to the next parcel issuing date five days away. The commander explained that some Red Cross consignments were shipped in bulk. In the issue was a tremendous cheese that must have been two feet in diameter by one foot high. This was cut into man-sized wedges. We all received a packet of tea, a can of powdered milk, a small can of mutton, a can of salmon, a few sugar cubes, a box of prunes, and a bar of what the British called Iron Ration, a hard chocolate bar somewhat similar to the U.S. government-issue D bar. To top it off, we each received two packs of cigarettes. My brands were Senior Service and Players. We also learned that the Germans supplemented the Red Cross food with a daily issue of either soup or boiled potatoes about evening time.

After relishing our finest meal in months, we lit up cigarettes. Feeling like expansive millionaires, we had a pleasant evening for the first time since capture. A couple of packs of cards materialized from somewhere, along with a harmonica and a checkerboard, and we all had a great time.

Wooden blackout shutters were put up to all the windows as dusk came, and we were cautioned that if we went to the john at night, or went from one barracks to another, to be extremely careful about lighting matches. That was one thing the Jerries were really tough about.

In talking with some of the old-timers, I found that in many ways, life in a prison camp was quite a bit like Civvy Street [civilian life]. There were various strata of prison camp society, and the camp had its capitalists, politicians, and poor.

Supper was no sooner completed than we were greeted by a host of salesmen. A typical example would be two soldiers coming through the barracks holding up a box of forty or fifty packs of cigarettes and selling chances for two cigarettes each. These, in the main, met with a rough reception from our newfound friend, the South African hut commander, who explained they sold many hundreds of these chances, and in some cases it was doubtful that the actual drawing ever took place. He termed them the camp parasites and contended they always tried to victimize newcomers.

Many boys also came in offering to exchange various foods for others. There was nothing wrong with this as long as we were satisfied that we had made a good deal, and we soon developed a good sense of value for this "stock exchange." With such a large camp, it was rumored that a few of the long-time inmates who were good horse traders had amassed some fabulous food hoards.

The hut commanders had almost unquestioned authority and were held strictly accountable for the proper conduct of their charges. In disciplinary cases, drumhead courts were held and the punishments doled out were severe indeed. We never found a hut commander who was not a square shooter, keenly conscious of his responsibilities.

The next morning we were accosted by several "blower" salesmen. A blower was a curious device made of empty tin cans cunningly shaped and joined together in a funnel arrangement and mounted on a board. At the intake end was a bladed propeller cut and formed from sections of tin, which was rotated by a wire or metal hand crank. This forced a blast of air through the horizontal run to an elbow and up to a wire grill. A few shavings of wood were placed on the grill, and then you turned the crank like mad. The idea was that you could boil up a can of water in a couple of minutes using a minimum of fuel. As the camp grounds were absolutely barren, it was clear that wood, or any combustible for that matter, was at a premium at *Stalag* VII A. These blowers were highly treasured possessions. It was amazing how ingenious the blower makers were. There were dozens of models, each maker claiming his was far superior to the competition. The boys spent days gleaning old tin cans, then laboriously cutting and pounding them with stones to shape them into their particular design. Each manufacturer had his own design concept and talked mysteriously of "Venturi effects" and even BTUs. To be a blower maker in a POW camp was to be a member of the elite of prison camp artisans.

Looking about the barracks, we could see that thousands had preceded us in a quest for kindling. The bunk bed uprights had yielded so many shavings and splinters that in many cases they were but half of their original dimensions, to the peril of the occupant of the uppermost bunk. Wood had been chipped from the floors and doors, and lucky was the fellow who boasted three bed slats.

Johnny and I decided we wouldn't buy a blower. First, we expected to be moved to an all-American camp in the not too distant future, so we wouldn't need to boil water for tea. Another, and better, reason was that it would have taken all of the food and cigarettes we had, and we had learned the hard way to hang on to our eats. As it turned out, there were some very friendly Scots next door who told us we could use their blower any time we wanted to brew up.

Johnny borrowed the blower, and I borrowed a rusty jackknife and set off to get some wood. Wandering through the barracks, I shaved off a splinter of wood from anything that looked as if it wouldn't collapse. The hut commander told us that stealing a bed slat was a serious offense, but it was considered cricket to take shavings wherever available. He perpetually got hell from the Jerries for this wood pilfering, or vandalism as they called it, but there was no point in issuing tea if the men had no way to prepare it.

In a few minutes, Johnny and I had the pot boiling. To the uninitiated, it was a strange sight out in back of the barracks that morning, dozens and dozens of soldiers crouched by their blowers, turning the cranks desperately. A few feet away, some Scots with asbestos throats gulped down boiling tea with steam still flying from the bubbling brew. It was April 1, and though the wind was cool, the sun promised warmth later in the day. The green fields way off in the distance sparkled with iridescent glory.

Next to us a soldier was operating one of the most unique blowers I had seen. It differed from the conventional models in that it had no propeller or hand crank. It was actuated by a spring about two and a half inches in diameter, over which paper had been affixed like a Japanese lantern. As the spring was alternately compressed and released, it functioned like a bellows.

After a good hot can of tea, we wandered around the barracks, meeting and chatting with prisoners of all nationalities. It was a lovely spring day, and everyone was outside enjoying the sunshine. From the older prisoners we found that *Stalag* VII A, except for the permanently assigned hut commanders and Allied supervisory personnel, was a transit camp, a sort of funnel through which all of the prisoners from Africa, Italy, Greece, and Yugoslavia passed on their way to permanent camp assignments. As this was long before the establishment of any second front, it meant that all Allied ground troops captured, with the exception of the Russians, passed through *Stalag* VII A at one stage or another. American prisoners were almost all eventually sent to camps in Pomerania, while the British generally wound up in East Prussia, Silesia, or Poland.

In the afternoon, while most of the boys were outside, we had quite a talk with our South African friend. He said postcards would be distributed that evening and we could write home to our folks, subject of course to normal censorship regulations and the exercise of common sense. The German censorship was not particularly severe, though obviously there could be no mention of place names or any implied criticism of the treatment we received. Prisoners were permitted to send one postcard and one letter weekly.

The South African, who had been captured during the debacle at Tobruk in 1942, said it had taken about four months to receive his first letter from his folks in Pretoria. Now he heard from home regularly and had received numerous parcels of food and clothing. The mail went via either Sweden or Switzerland, and this circuitous route was the main reason for the slow service.

Stalag VII A was assuredly the most cosmopolitan prison camp in existence. There must have been twenty nationalities represented, and we soon learned to identify all of the strange uniforms. South Africans could be spotted by the orange flash on the uniform shoulders, Scots by the Glengarry bonnets, and Serbs by their smart dove-gray uniforms and crimson hat tops. Also present in sizable numbers were Greeks, Cypriots, French, Belgians, Sikhs, Gurkhas, New Zealanders, Maoris, Australians, Russians, Poles, Palestinians, Canadians, Dutch, and Norwegians. There were even a few Italians, one or two of whom had been captured by the British in the desert and later freed by the Germans. Now they were in the unique position of being the prisoners of their former comrades in arms.

The Germans left us pretty much to our own devices, only periodically patrolling through the compound area and barracks. When the guards did enter barracks on inspection tours, they did all of their talking to the hut commanders, all of whom spoke and understood German well. This probably accounted for the fact that very many of the hut commanders were South Africans. German is similar to Afrikaans, which they all spoke since childhood.

The Germans mostly contented themselves with maintaining a strong guard around the camp perimeter. In addition to

the huge twenty-five-foot high barbed-wire barricade surrounding the camp, there was a lower barbed barricade about thirty
feet inside the outer fence. The space between the barricades
was a mass of huge coils of wire. The inner fence bore notices
warning that the guards in the towers were ordered to open
fire as soon as anyone stepped past the inner fence. Fifty-foot
towers extended high above the outer fence all along the outer
rim of the camp at intervals of 500 feet. These towers were
equipped with searchlights and machine guns and were
manned twenty-four hours a day. Outside the camp, armed
guards patrolled in pairs, often accompanied by a muzzled and
leashed Alsatian dog. It was a physical impossibility for any man
to get through the inner fence, work his way through coils of
wire, and then surmount the twenty-five-foot outer fence.
There was also a great dread of the dogs.

The German red-white-and-black flag flew from the flagpole at the camp entrance. A wide blacktopped road came
through the main gate and bisected the camp. Several lesser
roads led off the main stem at right angles. Clustered near the
main gate were the guards' sleeping quarters, kitchens, supply
warehouses, and various administration buildings. Right in the
middle of the road, at the gate, was a white-and-black diagonally striped sentry checkpoint. Every time I saw it, I thought of
the comic strip *Sentinel Louie*.

Mounted along the top of the outer fence were loudspeak-
ers, over which announcements were frequently made. Every
night at about six o'clock, as a sort of after-dinner treat, they
played fifteen minutes of martial band music, including such
favorites as the "Hohenfriedberger March" and "Deutschland,
Deutschland Über Alles." We were truly a captive audience.

Several barracks were for community use. One often held
amateur theatricals and concerts, while another served as the
church for Sunday services. The camp had many barbers, and
the going rate for a haircut was three cigarettes. In the evening
there were poker games, Canfield, a crude roulette wheel, and
even the pea-under-the-walnut game for those who were
tempted to gamble.

At five thirty each evening two men were sent down to the cookhouse with a galvanized tub to bring back our ration of boiled potatoes. These were golf ball–size, boiled in their skins and guaranteed cold on arrival. We normally wound up with three small spuds each.

On the fourth night after our arrival, an incident occurred that I will never forget for stark realism. Just after the potatoes had been distributed, the hut commander called for attention. Mounting a table, he spoke to the assembled barracks, stating that one of the boys sent to fetch the potatoes had been accused of filling his overcoat pockets on the way back to the barracks. The hut leader said that if this were a British soldier, he would have prescribed the disciplinary action, but as the accused was an American, he would disqualify himself from sitting in judgment and instead name a three-man American trial board.

The poor wretch huddled miserably by the table, the center of all attention, obviously not enjoying his role. As the trial commenced, the prosecutor angrily and scornfully accused the lad of stealing from his buddies and being a disgrace to the American uniform. The boy literally collapsed, sobbing in semi-hysteria. For all of us it was an embarrassing and humiliating moment. We couldn't condone what he had done, particularly as the British were such sticklers on discipline and punishment, yet I don't think there was one of us that did not feel a surge of pity for the boy. It was a tense moment. There was no need to continue the trial, for the boy shrieked out his guilt and cast himself on the mercy of his fellows. After some deliberation, it was decided that as he liked German potatoes so much that he would steal from his pals, he could do without the Red Cross parcel that would have been issued to him the following day. In a private conversation later on, the hut commander agreed that the course adopted had certainly been the right one, though he felt we had been exceptionally lenient. Though the loss of his parcel was a great privation, I know the lad would willingly have forgone his next three parcels could he have won back the esteem of his fellow prisoners. From that day on he was a pariah to his countrymen.

The next day we received our first Red Cross parcel issue. This was a Canadian parcel, the most highly regarded of all. They differed from the British, American, and Australian parcels in that they contained a pound of real Maple Leaf butter as opposed to margarine. Instead of the mutton in the New Zealand and Australian parcels, these had a can of Spam. The cigarettes were Sweet Caporals.

The longer we remained at *Stalag* VII A, the more we learned how well organized it was. There was a single-sheet mimeographed camp newspaper (no war news, just personal items, of course), a limited number of playing cards, checkers, chess sets, a fairly well-stocked library, frequent impromptu amateur-hour variety shows, a really top-notch dance band, and opportunities to enroll in correspondence courses given by the University of London, for which college credits were given. Church services were held every Sunday, including communion services. Sunday afternoon was given over to sports, and the French and Belgian soccer teams put on a spirited match my first Sunday at Moosburg. This was their national pastime, and they played with all the fervor of an International Cup match. I recall rooting for the Belgians, primarily because they were so outnumbered, but they lost 3–2 in the closing minutes.

It was interesting to see the various reactions and attitudes of the prisoners toward this life of enforced idleness. Many were skilled and devoted much of their time to devising ways of becoming more proficient at their chosen professions. A few were schoolteachers or experts in some commercial field, and these took great pleasure in conducting classes for students. An architect made a T square and drawing board and spent months sketching buildings, bridges, and other structures. Many of us were ardent readers and spent hours outside, backs against the barracks wall, lost in some fictional tale. There were, unfortunately, a lot of prisoners to whom none of these pursuits appealed. They seemed to make no effort to make the best of a bad situation and became morose and taciturn, obsessed by self-pity, their constant thought *How long, how long?* But even these could find some solace in letting their thoughts run to their loved ones.

One thing that impressed me greatly was the variety of licensed food-exchange huts. All of the commodities rates were posted on the wall in terms of cigarettes. For instance, a jar of Nescafé was rated at three packs of cigarettes, a box of prunes at fifteen cigarettes, a can of tuna or salmon at twenty cigarettes, etc. All straight food-for-food swaps were calculated in terms of cigarettes and change made accordingly. In this way anyone having a penchant for any given article could readily swap less desired items and stock up on his favorite. This worked out very well in tea and coffee, as the British preferred tea and the Americans usually would rather have the coffee. Similarly, many of the British preferred their Players cigarettes to our Camels.

Of course, the market would sometimes run out of stock on certain items or get too loaded with others, which forced a price adjustment. It was the age-old law of supply and demand in operation, with prices seeking their own level. The one item very seldom seen on the stock exchange shelves was the priceless Canadian Maple Leaf butter.

When the exchange did not have what you wanted, you took recourse to the black market, which was all that the name implies. The guards were strictly prohibited from trading with the prisoners, but it was common knowledge that many of them did. They all loved coffee, but this couldn't be had for love or money in Germany in those days. It was an odd situation, the prisoners enjoying one small luxury that their captors were denied. One night there was hell to pay in the barracks. One of the more enterprising GIs had traded a jar of Nescafé to a Jerry guard for five eggs. The gimmick that brought the house down was that the soldier had taken an empty coffee jar, filled it with the correct shade of brown dirt, and then added a quarter-inch layer of coffee on top for aroma and inspection purposes. When the guard went to savor his coffee in the privacy of his room, he must have blown a gasket. The guard was in a peculiar spot. He couldn't complain to the German officers, as he would be forced to admit that he had deliberately violated a basic rule. On the other hand, he was sufficiently rankled at being victimized that he didn't propose to take it lying down. Fuming and ranting, he came charging in to the hut leader and laid down an ultimatum. Either he got a jar of real coffee within an hour or he would make it rough on the lot of us. Of course the hut leader disclaimed any responsibility and said that if the Jerry would identify the soldier, he would see to it that the guard got his coffee. The hut leader was on safe ground in saying this, as he knew the guard could not identify the GI in question. Several facts made this apparent. First, the transaction took place outside long after dark. Second, we all looked pretty much alike, being identically uniformed. Thirdly, if the Jerry could have identified the soldier, he would have approached him directly and not gone to the hut leader. The ultimatum came and went and nothing happened. In the final analysis, it was the German who lost face. We knew he couldn't take the matter to a higher authority, and any punitive measures could only be ordered by a German officer. He did provide us with a lively topic of speculation for a few days.

Along sanitary lines, we were all given a small bar of soap and four razor blades during our first few days at *Stalag* VII A. Most of us had our GI razor kits with us when captured, and it was refreshing to hack off the six-week beards we all sported. A few of the boys were intrigued by their new creations and elected to keep their beards. Varieties of mustaches and goatees were groomed, though none of the mustaches were of the approved Führer toothbrush type. Some went in for handlebar models, and the Clark Gable misplaced–style of eyebrow enjoyed quite a vogue.

We stayed at *Stalag* VII A for eleven days. One afternoon about three o'clock an announcement came over the public address system that all American prisoners would move out the following day to a permanent camp. It was with some regret that we shook hands with our British buddies the next morning and lined up with our small bundles of food. One thing was certain: We were far better equipped and in much better physical and mental condition for this trip than for our four-day boxcar ordeal from La Torina through the Brenner Pass.

CHAPTER 5

Stalag II B, Hammerstein

The next morning, in a misting soft rain, we were lined up on the parade grounds and counted three or four times, amid much shouting and confusion. The Germans were even more dramatic than usual with their counting ritual. These incessant counts, coming with all the fanfare of a Hollywood production, seemed be the hallmark of the *Wehrmacht*. The senior officer would be up at the head of the group, each non-com would count his detachment, and then they would all converge on the head man and have a short huddle. Invariably, the resulting figure would be unsatisfactory, and the process would be repeated a couple of times more.

After taking about half an hour on average to verify the various head counts, we were ready to board the train and marched down to the railroad spur. Before boarding, we were each given a quarter loaf of bread to go with the remains of our parcel food. Loading arrangements were thirty to a boxcar, and with the nail keg privy reasonably braced in the center of the car, we set off with much lurching and whistle tooting.

The trip was a four-day journey with no untoward incidents and differed little from the trip taken from Italy except that we had a couple of extra water stops. As before, we squinted through a crack in the sidewall, which we enlarged somewhat with a jackknife. At least twice we were held over for long waits in large marshaling yards. Knowing our starting point and ultimate destination, I am inclined to think that these halts were probably in the cities of Prague and Breslau.

After about twenty stops, just when we were imagining we must have reached the outskirts of Moscow, the train squealed to a halt, the doors were thrown open, and we hobbled out. This was the end of the line, for us at least. It was about noontime. Blinking our eyes to get accustomed to the glare of daylight again, we saw we had debarked only a few hundred feet from a cement country railroad station labeled HAMMERSTEIN.

This was a pastoral scene if ever there was one. The station, as in a great many German villages, was quite a way removed from the village proper. We were surrounded by fields, and we were most impressed by the sparkling green of the landscape. A real County Cork green, it seemed, though no doubt the fact that we had been in virtual pitch blackness for four days made the color seem more vivid than it actually was.

The land was almost devoid of trees and flat as a billiard table. I can recall thinking what a dream of a place it would be for engineers commissioned to lay out an airport. All they would have needed was some asphalt. The guards were as pleased as we were to have arrived, so without much fuss we formed ranks and marched three miles to our new home, *Stalag* II B, Hammerstein, Pomerania.

Nearing the camp, we saw that while the barbed wire, buildings, towers, and other physical features were in keeping with the accepted prison camp format, this place was very much smaller than *Stalag* VII A. This was as expected, for we knew this camp was occupied almost solely by Americans.

After the usual checklist, sign, countersign, and the rest of the mumbo-jumbo at the gate, we passed inside to an area immediately in front of the camp administration building. Our arrival had created quite a stir in the camp. Well over a thousand GIs crowded out of the barracks to get a look at the new arrivals. They kept a respectful distance, as our guards were very much in evidence. Entering the building in single file, we were told to display our metal identity plates while the data was transcribed onto cards.

When the last man had emerged, we were turned over to a GI sergeant who led us through the jam of old-timers to our assigned barracks. There were about 650 of us in the group, and four complete barracks had been cleaned out to receive us. Each barracks housed about 125 men, so the surplus were placed in other barracks not completely full. As soon as we had been allotted bunk space and issued palliasses, we were told that the next day was parcel-issue day, and then were left on our own.

The old-timers paraded through in force, shouting out their hometowns and divisions, searching for anyone with a common background. The barracks resounded to shouts of "Any Texans here?," "Who's from Pittsburgh?," or "Anybody from the 34th Division?" When they located boys from their neck of the woods, they got into a long-winded check of place names, hometown gin mills, and mutual interests. DiCrecchio and I were staggered to find in this crew a New Haven boy, Nick D'Errico, who had shared our barracks back at Camp Croft during basic training. Although this was a scant nine months removed, it seemed like we had all lived three lifetimes in the interim. Nick had been with the 3rd Division and had been taken on the heights in the Montecassino sector about five weeks before our capture. He had been overrun while on outpost duty. Nick picked up a severe case of frostbitten feet en route to the German rear area.

Nick had been at *Stalag* II B for two months, and gave us the lowdown on all phases of *Stalag* life. Religious services in all major faiths were held each Sunday at the converted barracks that served as a chapel. About twice a month there were variety entertainments featuring the *Stalag* band. This band was made up predominantly of GIs, but there were a few French and Belgians at the camp, and four of these were excellent musicians. One Belgian, in particular, played as good a tenor sax as I have ever heard.

Nick played drums and, knowing that I had been a sax player prior to my army days, he invited me to sit in on a couple of their rehearsals. I was surprised to see the top-notch arrangements and fine instruments, all new, provided by the Red Cross. Unfortunately, my playing was not good enough to secure band membership, which I had known before I tried out. The leader was a GI who had played with Bernie Cummins and other name bands.

The camp library was always available, and this proved a blessing to those of us who took a keen delight in reading. The selections were many and varied, and I could always find something of interest on the shelves. Of course there were a few clinkers, such as *Beekeeping in the Orkney Islands* or *Mating Habits of the Arctic Tern,* but these were in the minority and were passed over by the discerning reader. There were several British novels about life in the old American West. These volumes, which probably passed muster in Mayfair, were simply uproarious, particularly when the sheriff, or "gunslinger" as the case might be, hitched his horse to a cottonwood tree, brewed himself a pot of tea, and loaded his conversation with Cockney colloquialisms. All of the books bore the stamp of the German censor, *Geprüft* (approved), on the flyleaf.

I think the highlight of my stay at *Stalag* II B was when I picked a copy of *You Can't Do Business with Hitler* stamped *Geprüft* off the shelf. This brought me as close to complete hysteria as I have ever been. I can only surmise that it must have been the regular censor's day off, or else he had as distorted a sense of humor as I had.

As far as food went, we had our weekly Red Cross parcel, supplemented by a German issue of ersatz coffee (tasted like roasted acorns), weekly loaf of rye bread, and daily issue of watery potato soup. Looking back, I can't remember ever having an issue of salt. I guess, with the exception of the daily soup, we lived on a salt-free diet.

There were occasional issues of small bars of soap and razor blades, and once a week we were permitted the luxury of a hot shower in the delousing building. The Germans were keenly interested in lice, it seemed, for in the entrance hall of the delousing building was a lecture hall chart showing a louse in all his glory magnified several million times. He was about as big as a washtub, and the German names of his various parts, all identified with arrows, were just about as long as the chart. It was not the type of picture to grace a living room wall.

We had few direct dealings with our captors. The camp was very efficiently run and was staffed with a good cadre of non-coms and a few officers who took over all direct contact with the enemy. A colonel was nominally in charge of the GIs, though I don't recall ever seeing him. The only officer I remember was a captain who served as chaplain and had a lot to do with organizing the little entertainment shows.

The weather was generally fair and getting warmer as we were now well into spring. After our morning toilet, a Spartan one, we lined up for the daily head count, and from then on the day was our own. Normally we all went outside, sat on the sandy ground with our backs propped against the barracks wall, and chatted with our neighbors or plunged into a book. Except for the men in the searchlight and machine-gun towers, and an occasional pair patrolling outside the wire, our guards were not much in evidence. These guards were by no means the flower of the German Army; they were a motley crew of old men and invalid veterans going through a period of semiconvalescence before going up to the front again. They all knew when they were well off, comparatively speaking, and did not harass us or provoke any incidents as long as we didn't kick over the traces. Looking them over, it was readily apparent that the Jerries were even then scraping the bottom of the manpower barrel.

We knew relatively few German words, certainly not enough to engage in a conversation, even if we were so minded. I was greatly surprised one day, while alone in a corner of the parade grounds, to have a guard come up, nod, and say hello. As I stared at him, he told me that he had worked as a plumber's helper in Philadelphia for fourteen years before returning to Germany in 1935. He had received bad leg wounds during a tour of duty on the Russian front, giving him a pronounced limp and a certainty of no more combat duty. He cautioned me to be discreet about our conversation, as his superiors did not look with favor on fraternization of any kind except in the normal line of duty. From then on, we made it a point to meet every couple of days for a short chat of a minute or two. He bore us no malice, and indeed said that he had been a damned fool to have left Philly, and wouldn't have had it not been for the Depression. One thing was sure, he had his bellyful of fighting, and grievous as his injuries were, I think he considered them a fair price to pay for transfer from the bleak Russian duty to the relative luxury of Pomerania. Of course, I fostered the acquaintanceship with a couple of cigarettes.

After I had been at *Stalag* II B for two weeks, the guard, Erich by name, told me that the camp was besieged with requests from the farms in the area for free prison labor and that within the next week, most able-bodied prisoners would be sent to the outlying districts in a *Kommando* (working party). It was Erich's opinion that this was much to be preferred to being cooped up at *Stalag* II B.

Back in the barracks, I had the story confirmed in a couple of hours by our noncom hut leader. The noncom said that the only way to avoid the draft was to come down "sick," and that the hospital personnel would back up, to the best of their ability, all who took this course. Actually, under international law only privates could be assigned to working parties of this nature, though noncoms, if they chose, could volunteer. The work was supposed to have absolutely no connection with the war effort, though it was difficult to see how any work in Germany was not related to the war effort in some way. Even if we were put to work making lace doilies, were we not freeing other persons to take a direct part in the war? It was a question that would have baffled a panel of jurists, and we were sure the Germans were not going to go into academic arguments.

Johnny DiCrecchio and I sought out a couple of the old-timers who had previously been out on *Kommando* and because of illness or other reasons returned to the *Stalag*. They left us under no illusions as far as hard work was concerned, but pointed out there were compensations in that we would have more freedom of movement and could supplement our diet with farm produce. These work groups were generally composed of fifteen or twenty men, one of whom was chosen leader, or *Vertrauensmann.* The English translation was "go-between." This person acted as spokesman for the group in its dealings with the farm authorities.

We also learned that although most of these work parties were for farm labor, it was possible that we could be sent to the coal mines, railroad yards, or any other line of endeavor that suited the Jerries' purpose. That was the chance we had to take. Johnny and I quickly decided that going on *Kommando* was for us. Going a step further, we realized that this group could be out for a long period of time and that it would only be common sense for us to see that our group was made up of boys we liked and respected. Within a couple of hours, we had made up a list of thirteen other lads whose sentiments were the same as ours. That this was probably the wisest move we made at Hammerstein is borne out by the fact that in our subsequent year, on the farm and on the march, not once was there any serious dissension or argument. Everyone on our handpicked list was always ready to do his share—and part of his buddy's if the need arose.

To illustrate this point, let me say that when Jess McDonald received the first civilian parcel from home, while on the farm, he commenced to divide it among us without a word. To show the spirit of the rest, they all refused his gift, saying, "Jess, your mother sent that to you." This altruism, mind you, came at a time when men of lesser moral fiber would have thrown ethics to the winds and been almost prepared to slit throats for the delicacies at stake. On our list, in addition to Johnny and me, were Jess McDonald and Ray Kudloski of Detroit; John Benson and Jim McLean from Chicago; Swede Olson of Antigo, Wisconsin; Hank Conlin of Minetto, New York; Steve Osak and John Estock from Pittsburgh; William Halvorsen from Iowa; Daniel Henderson from Virginia; Arch Blevins from Beckley, West Virginia; Chester Stough from York, Pennsylvania; Harlynt Robinson from Ohio; Elmer Eagle from Droop, West Virginia; Delbert Kinder from Morehead, Kentucky; and Jim Pierce, and Bill Walters, whose hometowns elude me. When the list was completed, we asked for an audience with the camp *Arbeits-führer,* or labor supervisor, who was somewhat surprised and pleased at our request.

The next day we were told to pack up, for we were going out on *Kommando* to a small village called Benzin. Just before we left, we had a small meeting in the barracks, and I was chosen *Vertrauensmann.* I remember thanking the boys for the trust they were showing in me and promising to do my best to see that we fared as well as possible.

Next morning, possessions bundled up, we reported to the *Arbeitsführer.* A stiff breeze was blowing and sandy dust was eddying in little whirls just above the parade ground as we walked over to the checkout point. We were given four Red Cross parcels each and assured by the issuing GI that before our supply was exhausted, we would be given opportunity to secure a three-month replenishment stock. The Red Cross office for our area was in a city called Stolp, and I was to report there to a man named Jack Schick for parcel supplies, clothing, and medical assistance, or to report any situation that needed a higher-level solution. Schick was to be our boy for contact purposes and grievances as well as books and whatever else was available from Red Cross stocks.

Our guard was a ruddy-faced private of about thirty-two who had lost an eye in combat. Seemingly in good spirits, he brought up the rear on our trek to the Hammerstein railway station. Aboard the train, it felt strange to be sitting in the passenger compartments again. Like all European railway cars, it was compartmented, with the aisle at the extreme side of the carriage. The seats were wooden benches, unpadded, but a 1,000-percent improvement over traveling via boxcar. Rolling along through green fields and pine forests, we were impressed with the cleanliness and beauty of the countryside. The civilians who passed through our carriage were mostly farm folk and gave us scant attention. Apparently GI uniforms were no rarity in this part of Germany.

After riding for about an hour, we came to a fair-sized city with a relatively pretentious station, where quite a few passengers boarded the train during our five-minute halt. I gave an inquiring look to the guard. Knowing I was the spokesman, he grunted, "Stolp."

All in all, the guard did not strike us as being a bad fellow. Once or twice he tried to get a conversation started, but the language barrier was too great. Some fifteen minutes out of Stolp, he gestured that we were to collect our gear and be ready to leave the train. A minute or two later the train pulled into a neat little station sitting amid a cluster of about a dozen houses. The station sign said BENZIN. Our guide herded us into a corner of the small but scrupulously clean station, and then launched into a loud harangue with a small man, replete with Führer-model mustache, who glittered in the most lavish uniform I have ever seen. This outfit would have put any field marshal or Park Avenue doorman to shame. A chocolate-brown-and-fawn two-tone job, it was of sumptuous broadcloth lavishly brocaded, complete with gold frogging and epaulettes. The most ludicrous note was the dress sword and scabbard, which our uniformed friend had to hoist up occasionally to keep it from dragging on the floor. We were later to find that this uniform went with the arduous job of being *Bahnhof Meister,* or station master, of this whistle-stop country station. Probably the uniform was calculated to do enough for the wearer's ego that he would not carp about the insignificant pay that went with the job. We were all properly in awe and marveled at our guard's effrontery in shouting so violently at this obvious VIP.

It turned out the guard was incensed because the farm had not sent a wagon for us, so we were confronted with a walk of six kilometers. After waiting for fifteen minutes, the guard put a good face on the matter, and we set off for our new home at a brisk pace in a column of threes. The guard was at the head of the line and, being unencumbered, was striding right along. We kept up for a couple of miles, but the heat of the day and the weight of our 50-pound Red Cross cartons and personal gear soon had us puffing. The gap between the head and rear of the column widened perceptibly.

Just when a few of us in the rear ranks were about ready to holler "Uncle," a farm wagon drawn by a pair of horses came around a bend in the road. This was the wagon the guard had been expecting, but for some reason it had been delayed en route. It was only a matter of minutes to toss the Red Cross cartons on the wagon, and we were ready to walk unburdened the rest of the way to our new home, a village and gigantic collective farm called Benzin.

PART TWO

Forced Labor

CHAPTER 6

Initial Impressions of Benzin

Now that we had lightened our load, we were able to catch our breath and take notice of our surroundings. From my own point of view, the rest of the walk to Benzin was through the prettiest bit of country I had seen since landing in Europe. Now the farmhouses were more closely located, and on the right was a wonderful brick and half-timbered inn sporting the sign GASTHAUS (hotel or tavern). Our guard halted the column while he went inside. Ostensibly he was asking directions, but more likely he was hoisting a stein of beer and checking the dimensions of the barmaid, as the place was to become the center of his social life for the next few months.

The lad driving the team, a boy of about fifteen, looked at us with unabashed curiosity. Pointing to himself, he said "Hans." He was affably inclined, and we cemented the relationship with a cigarette. Old-timers who had briefed us on *Kommando* procedure had told us the value of a judiciously given cigarette, and in the months ahead we were to learn how right they were.

After fifteen minutes the guard reemerged and piloted us another mile to a small brick building surrounded by barbed wire, which was surely tagged as our new home away from home. Outside the building were two or three girls, a couple of old men, and the *Inspektor*, a giant of a man with a unique appearance. He was a full six feet four inches tall and proportionately wide. Myopic eyes peered from behind tortoiseshell-rimmed glasses on a moonlike face, red to the point that one thought of apoplexy just looking at him. His clothing was equally bizarre—a belted Norfolk jacket, tight-kneed schoolboy knickers, a stiff Herbert Hoover collar, and riding boots, topped off by a hunting crop. The hat, a green fedora, brim down all the way around, had a miniature shaving brush affixed to the hatband.

From the bull-like roar that came from him as we hove into view, it appeared he really did suffer from apoplexy. The tirade began when we were a couple of hundred feet away, and even when we were right next to him it did not diminish one whit. Pacing back and forth, hunting crop flicking constantly, he unburdened himself for a full six minutes to everybody within earshot, and if the wind was right, that might have included the *Bahnhof Meister* four miles back up the road. When he finally paused for breath, the guard got in a few words and, peering around *Herr Inspektor*, bellowed "*Vertrauensmann, VERTRAUENSMANN!*"

Stepping forward nervously, I pointed to myself, indicating that I was the *Vertrauensmann*. This touched off another three-minute outburst, punctuated by much pounding of his fist in the palm of his hand and the constant waggling of a banana-sized finger about an inch from my nose. I think John L. Lewis, eyebrows and all, would have quailed before this character. Anything I could have said would have been ineffectual, and as I hadn't understood a word spoken I just stood there, confirming, no doubt, his apparent impression that I was indeed dumb. It was not an auspicious beginning for my new career as *Vertrauensmann*. One thing was sure, we knew who was boss at Benzin.

During this display of temperament, the old men and the girls had been quite amused. Suddenly the *Inspektor* grinned, motioned us to go into the wire-enclosed yard, and left with the guard. In our later associations with the *Inspektor* we were to learn that he roared and dramatized in this manner even in commenting on the weather, but at this moment we were a pretty subdued bunch with a single thought: *What have we let ourselves in for?*

Left alone for twenty minutes, we examined our new surroundings with a great deal of interest. We were to be housed

in a brick building 36 feet long by 18 feet wide. Formerly it had
housed pigs, but it had been newly whitewashed inside, with
ten two-bunk beds placed in a row against the far wall. The
doorway was in the absolute center of the building, with one
window on each side halfway between the doorframe and the
building corner. The furnishings were Spartan: a cold water
tap and wooden washtub on a shelf, a cement oven and stove,
one long eating table flanked by two benches, and a single
naked electric lightbulb suspended by a cord from the ceiling.
The barbed wire took off from each end of the building, forming a 180-degree semicircle pierced by a wooden gate. The
small yard enclosed by the wire contained a two-hole privy.

The guard, apparently having been shown his room at the
Inspektor's house, returned with two civilian overseers, who
directed six of us to bring straw into the barracks for our beds
in the bunk bed frames. This done, we were left alone for
another quarter hour before the guard returned with a German of about sixty who spoke fairly good English and also had
some knowledge of French. He was introduced as Paul Mahn,
and he explained that he had acquired his knowledge of
English as an Allied prisoner in World War I. We were told we
could select one man, either permanently or on a rotating
basis, as cook. This man would be given foodstuffs each morning by the *Inspektor*'s *Frau*, or wife. In addition to preparing our
noon and evening meals, keeping the barracks clean, and splitting kindling for the stove, the cook would be expected to per-
form some small duties at the main house.

We would be aroused each morning at 5:20 by the *Wach-
mann* (guard), who would return at 6:00, at which time we
were to line up in the yard. Every morning two or three overseers would select as many men as they required for the particular job they had at hand.

Obviously proud of his linguistic ability and the rapt attention from an interested audience, Paul Mahn talked to us for
over an hour. We found that he was particularly vulnerable
as far as cigarettes were concerned, and he gave us a great deal
of valued information that would have taken weeks to learn

otherwise. It was his opinion that some of us would show an aptitude for certain types of work and be permanently assigned to specific duties, rather than remain in the labor pool.

Before the war, Benzin had been one huge baronial estate. The estate was more than 5,000 acres, and the entire village of Benzin had been in the employ of the baron. The one exception was the proprietor of the *Gasthaus*, who represented the only free enterprise in the village. The local residents had all worked for the baron on a wage basis, and over a period of time had been permitted to purchase small holdings about their homes, which they farmed on weekends exclusively for themselves.

This was all changed now. Collectivized by government edict into a mammoth state farm, Benzin was operated primarily on behalf of the *Wehrmacht*. The government seizure of the Baron's lands had engulfed the private holdings in the same fell swoop, and in a trice the local people's status had changed from voluntary paid laborers to almost serfs or indentured servants. They were forbidden by law to seek employment elsewhere or to request to leave the area. They no longer owned their lands and dwellings, and instead of a receiving wages they now worked on a sort of sharecropping basis. All this was necessary for the interests of the Fatherland, of course, and it would have been unpatriotic, if not treasonable, to protest.

With the government seizure, *Herr Inspektor*, fresh from agricultural college in Berlin, had come to run the show. The *Inspektor* called all of the shots and even had judicial powers over Benzin residents. He was also the local Nazi Party chairman, so his power was almost absolute.

The *Inspektor* was given quotas to fill for the *Wehrmacht* in all phases of farm production. The quotas were pegged as high as 92 percent of any given crop raised under the most ideal conditions, and woe betide the *Inspektor* and his lackeys if quotas were not met. Let us say, for example, that the rye quota was 100,000 bushels, and thanks to good weather, 109,000 bushels were harvested. The *Wehrmacht* got their 100,000 bushels first, and theoretically the 9,000-bushel surplus was distributed on a per capita basis among the workers. The apportionment was on a scale of one and a half shares per male overseer, one share per adult other than an overseer, and a half share per child over five and under fifteen years of age. We got the impression, however, that there was some chicanery in this regard on the *Inspektor*'s part, and if there was a reasonable surplus, by some fast double-entry bookwork the lion's share of it would go to his personal account. Knowing his stature and having met the man, it was hard to conceive of anyone seriously challenging his bookkeeping.

To be fair about it, I must admit that the *Inspektor* was under terrific pressure from his superiors, and it is somewhat understandable that after a severe reaming from his army bosses, he would take it out on whoever was handiest. Their demands were ever increasing. The choleric old bastard could read the riot act with more gusto than any person I ever met, before or since, and that includes a lot of "old army" sergeants who had made reaming people out their life's work.

The *Inspektor* had inherited a motley crew to work the farm. The nucleus of his workforce were a few native German men aged fifty-five or over, a few adult women, about fifteen girls in their teens, and a few boys in the twelve to fifteen age group. To bolster this nucleus, he had six Ukrainian girls working as forced laborers, eight Frenchmen, and his new twenty-man American crew of "farm experts." It was clear that his plans hinged in great measure on our performance, or lack of it, and the dramatic tirade when we arrived must have been his version of a Knute Rockne "Get in there and fight" speech.

The "Uke" girls were only about sixteen or seventeen, but despite their short stature, they must have tipped the scales at an average of 170 pounds. They could lift 150-pound grain sacks with ease, and they would have caught the eye of any Notre Dame line coach. This work was no transition to them. They were an impassive, stolid crew, and although they seemed friendly, they never had much to say.

Then there were the eight Frenchmen on the farm. Frenchmen were always somewhat suspect, to both GIs and British, as there were among them, so to speak, "two different breeds of cats." On the one hand—and these were in the minority—there were the French soldiers taken in the early days of the war when there was a Maginot Line. These were all pretty much good fellows, though prone to be defeatists as far as the war outcome was concerned. There was also a large group of French volunteer laborers who came to work in Germany expecting to enjoy a fuller dinner pail, because eating was not so good in France. Others said they were forced to come. A very great number came because they were opportunists and wanted to be found riding the right horse at the end of the race. In this latter group—and they numbered into the hundreds of thousands— were many who had been the backbone of the Hitlerite fifth column, men who had sold their country down the river.

Because they had been in Germany so long, the Frenchies, both former army personnel and turncoat civilians, were not considered a threat, so they were given a great deal of personal liberty. They were not locked in, had no guard, and as long as they showed up for work every morning seemed almost their own masters.

The Ukrainian girls, who occupied a room around the corner from us in the same building, also had very little surveillance. They were friendly in their own way, and though they showed no vivacity or mental prowess, their hearts were in the right place. As a general rule they spoke little, and I think this was shyness as much as anything else. After we had been at Benzin for a couple of weeks, we found that they would mend socks and do little sewing jobs for us, as well as washing and ironing. We all got a big kick out of the flatiron, though we had to admit it did an excellent job. It was as large as a shoebox and actually was nothing more than a metal receptacle for hot coals. Of course we always gave them a chocolate bar, though they did similar chores for the Frenchies with no thought of repayment. I believe they felt that we, the Frenchies, and they were all akin in the sense that we were anti-German, and in their way of thinking the jobs they did for us were rightfully women's work. Three of our boys—Estock, Osak, and

Kudloski—spoke fluent Polish, Ukrainian, and Croat, and through them we could secure information from the girls.

At six o'clock on our first day at Benzin, the *Inspektor* showed up with the guard and opened a small storeroom around the corner from our living quarters, where we piled up the twenty cartons of Red Cross parcels that we'd brought with us from *Stalag* II B. This done, the *Inspektor* made quite a ceremony of locking the door, showed me the key, and advised that when we wanted parcels he would come and open the storeroom for us.

He had either had an excellent supper or had been reading up on labor relations, for I never saw him mellower than that evening. He was almost coy. Dismissing the guard, he motioned me toward his house. Once inside, he nodded to his wife, a rather pleasant-featured blonde woman, who, in the hesitating manner of one speaking a language long unused, said hello. I was agreeably surprised to find that she spoke English, and as her confidence returned, she said it had been a part of her school studies but she had very few opportunities to use it.

The *Inspektor* had gone into the kitchen, returning with three glasses of a white wine. From this point on, his wife took over as interpreter. From the turn the conversation took, it was apparent that the *Inspektor* wanted to get a line on the capabilities of his new farmhands. His first question was "What is your name?" Realizing that Jack might be difficult for him to pronounce, I answered "Johann." This met with a nod and an indication of approval and prompted the second question, *"Du bist Deutsch, nein?"* (You're German, aren't you?) When I shook my head and said *"Engländer,"* he looked a little disappointed.

He launched into a series of questions about the boys. I told him that I was familiar with most of them and that at least six—Delbert Kinder, Daniel Henderson, William Halvorsen, Hank Conlin, Elmer Eagle, and Jim Pierce—were farm boys who presumably would fit right in with the work at hand. The oldest of our crew was Swede Olson, a pulpwood cutter with a long background of farm and ranch work. Of the rest, a couple had been factory machine operators, I had been a clerical worker, and the rest were students fresh from high school.

From his expression as I talked, it was clear that the first seven case histories were up to snuff, but he obviously was not overly elated about the rest of us. After a bit of a pep talk along the lines that he expected a good day's work out of each and every one of us, and the old routine that if we served him well he would be fair with us, he informed me that I would be held personally accountable for any shortcomings that developed. I would be allowed to go to Red Cross headquarters in Stolp about once a month, and in case of any serious illness or accident, our boys could go to the *Lazarette* (medical clinic) at Stolp for treatment.

The audience over, the *Inspektor* walked me back to the barracks. It was now quite dark. He cautioned us to be sure to put up the wooden window shutters each night, counted us, and locked us in. He brought an alarm clock that was set at 5:15 A.M. and left on the community table. We had naturally expected him to lock the outer gate, but not until he was outside the building did we realize that he had also locked the door of the barracks. There would be no access to the privy until 5:30 the next morning. Then and there we decided that this would be the first concession the *Vertrauensmann* would work on. The second item on the list was to get him to replace the 25-watt lightbulb with something that would throw out a little illumination. The lightbulb we had inherited had all the power of last year's Christmas tree bulb.

Scouting around a bit, we saw that the stove was a simple cement-enclosed firebox with two round cast-iron top plates. Next to it was a small pile of split kindling, to be replenished as needed by the cook. The stove was going to be adequate from a cooking standpoint. How much heat it would throw out was problematic, but we wouldn't have to worry about that until October, and a lot could happen between now and then. The cold water tap at the far end of the room was topped by a small grimy mirror. On a wall shelf, directly under the tap, was a wooden basin, along the lines of a butter firkin, for morning ablutions. For kitchen implements, there were twenty tin pie plates, a saucepan, a frying pan, a 10-quart galvanized pail, and an odd assortment of knives, spoons, and forks.

Our bed was a wooden framework box approximately six feet high, suspended within a framework of two-by-fours. The beds had been filled with straw after we arrived. At *Stalag* II B, we had each drawn two GI blankets, and for a pillow we rolled up our shirt or pants. Before leaving the *Stalag*, we had each been issued a new pair of GI shoes, three pairs of socks, one spare shirt, a toothbrush, and a small German-English paperback dictionary, and a few of the boys had been lucky enough to pick up a GI overcoat.

I had the most bizarre costume of the bunch. While at *Stalag* VII A, the Germans had given me a blue overcoat with brass buttons. The collar and cuffs were black velvet with red piping. On the tips of the lapels was a red velvet insignia reading "57." On the coat sleeves were four gold bars. A matching blue hat completed the ensemble. I kept this outfit for fifteen months, and on the day I discarded it the mothball aroma was as strong as the day I received it. I was speechless when they handed it to me, not because I scorned it, but because not in the screwiest musical comedy had I ever seen anything to equal it. The British at *Stalag* VII A—and this was later confirmed by the Benzin Frenchies—assured me that it was a French artillery officer's coat, vintage about 1870, doubtless taken as booty during the Franco-Prussian War by the forward-looking Teutons of that day for just such an occasion as this. There were several hundred of these coats issued at *Stalag* VII A, but none with the braid and adornments that mine had. The outfit certainly had individuality, and I took a perverse pride in the outlandish costume. At times I even pondered on the possibility that coats like this one might have been worn at such famous battles as Marengo or Austerlitz.

Knowing that a grueling day was coming up, and somewhat tuckered from our afternoon hike, we all turned in by 9:50 P.M. The alarm went off like a banshee the next morning. Tumbling out of bed, we all woke up in a hurry as we sloshed the icy water from the bucket over our faces and hands. Bill Walters had been named the cook the night before, and having lit the fire about a half hour before we got up, he soon had a potful of boiling water ready. We all had some Nescafé in our Red Cross parcels, and after a cup of steaming coffee we were ready to go when the guard shrilled his whistle for the morning lineup in the yard.

CHAPTER 7

Work Details

In the gray half-light of early morning we waited while three overseers picked their crews for the day. One wore a flat-visored taxicab-driver hat and the accepted Hitler mustache. We came to know him as "Potato Pop." He generally had a pretty good-sized crew and had nominal charge of the potato, turnip, and sugar beet details. Paul Mahn, our confidant of the night before, seemed to be the big wheel in the rye, hay, and ensilage departments. The third man of the trio, a quiet, red-faced man called Heinrich, was in charge of the tree-felling and lumbering gang. After these three had made their selections, only Conlin, Henderson, and I were left. The *Inspektor* latched on to Conlin and Henderson, brought them to the stables, and assigned them teams of horses. From then on they were teamsters.

After the groups were assigned, they would go to the tool shed to be given the tools for the day—hoes, pitchforks, shovels, or what have you—and then were led by the overseer out to the fields. The guard invariably went with the largest of the work details, which was generally Potato Pop's.

The woods gang left their axes, saws, and wedges buried under pine boughs each night when they left work, so they had no tools to carry. On Saturdays the woodsmen, on their way back to the barracks, always left their axes at the blacksmith's for sharpening and picked them up on their way to the woods Monday mornings.

For the first few days, either because of my rank or because I may have looked as if I would not be much use in the fields, I was assigned to Franz Mahn, a brother of Paul, who was the general maintenance man for the farm. Franz's workshop was in the same building as our barracks, around the corner and separated from our room by the quarters of the Uke maidens. He set me to work shaping axe handles and fork handles. It was always amazing to see him take a rough-sawed shape and in a short space of time fashion it with a draw knife and smaller scraping tools into a first-class handle. He was very patient with me and explained, as well as we could converse, about the grain of the wood, the point of balance, and many other features that distinguish a good fork handle from a poor one. By the time noon rolled around and I went back to join Walters for lunch, I had picked up at least twenty-five new German words. Most of these were the names of tools, which Franz would repeat over and over. By working alone with the German, I was in a position to make more rapid strides in the language than the others, who were working in groups and were not so absolutely reliant on the foreign tongue as I was. My first few handles were pretty crude, but Franz seemed satisfied with my efforts. Indeed, once or twice he came over and complimented me on a job well done. As maintenance men, we took on a variety of chores daily such as glazing window frames, oiling the pump, and even some wiring. For a man with little formal schooling and few tools to work with, Franz was really very competent in practically any kind of carpentry work and electrical repairs. Franz even designed parts to keep our one old tractor going.

I reported to the workshop about 6:15 every morning, and at 10:00 A.M. Franz would knock off for about twenty minutes. During this period, I would go back to the barracks for a cup of Nescafé. At 1:00 P.M. we would halt for half an hour, and then I would have a bowl of Walters's soup of the day, which was always simmering on the stove from noontime through 6:30 in the evening. Those of us working close to the barracks would have soup both at lunchtime and in the evening, while those working more than a mile away took a sandwich or heel of bread and piece of cheese to the fields with them to tide them over until night.

In the mornings, Walters swept out the barracks and split a supply of kindling, then went over to the *Inspektor*'s kitchen for the daily food handout. This was usually a good lot of small cull potatoes and a turnip or two. Once in a while we would be lucky and the soup would have a third ingredient, usually peas, carrots, radishes, or an onion. The cooking was quite simple: fill one large black pot two-thirds with water and add potatoes (preferably peeled), sliced turnip, and whatever else you might have. Bring to a boil, add salt, and let simmer all day. Frequently we would have our soup at noon, and then use our parcel food for the evening meal. Although it would have been thriftier to take soup both times, it really wasn't that good.

On Saturdays we were each given a loaf of rye bread from the village bake house, next to the smithy. This was a solid loaf with a crust that would blunt a hacksaw blade. Though it did not have much taste appeal, it was certainly filling. A couple of slabs of this with a slice of corned beef or cheese in between would hold off the hunger pangs for quite a spell.

Having by this time acquired a distinct aversion to potato soup, many of us preferred for Walters to save us some raw potatoes, which we would slice and fry with our Red Cross margarine. The only trouble here was that when ten of us decided on fried spuds for supper, the one with the last turn at the frying pan had a real late supper.

Under Franz Mahn's guidance, I was becoming more proficient daily. Now I undertook an ambitious project: fashioning a yoke for oxen from a solid block of wood. Franz had a model handy and a pair of calipers to make measurement comparisons. It was a slow job with the primitive tools at our disposal.

Franz had been working on a pair of wagon wheel hubs for which I was shaving the spokes. The metal wheel treads were made in two sections, and when the rest of the wheels were finished, we brought the assemblies down to the village smithy to install the treads. Gustave Topel, the blacksmith, was a friendly, whiskered old fellow liked by all. He fanned and heated to cherry red the metal retaining bands that were to girdle the rims of the wheels. Setting the bands over the wooden circles, we heaved pails of water on the assemblies. The metal sent up clouds of steam as it contracted, biting into the wooden wheel rim in a permanent bond. The wood groaned under the stress. After they had cooled off, we stood them up and rolled them along, real perfect circles. I am amazed to this day that it was possible to make wheels more than four feet in diameter in this manner and have them come out so well, especially with the shrinking and other factors to be considered.

After a week of working with Franz, my German had increased by leaps and bounds. I was adding some thirty or forty new words to my vocabulary daily without conscious effort. The same was true of the rest of the boys, and by pooling our knowledge we now had little difficulty making ourselves understood except on technical or abstract matters. Franz displayed a lively curiosity about America, and I did my best to answer him truthfully and satisfactorily. For his part, he was cooperative and went to great lengths to explain things that to my eyes seemed strange.

Immediately after my election as the *Vertrauensmann* back at the *Stalag*, I laid down the policy that in our talks with the Jerries we would steer clear of all topics related to the war, who was wrong, who was right, who would win, etc. The Germans also seemed eager to stay away from such controversial topics. Peculiar as it seems, never once in our ten months at Benzin was any topic brought up that led to recriminations or harsh words, either by our captors or ourselves. As each successive day passed, our band of GIs, by their dependability, friendliness, and good work, were creating a wealth of goodwill among all those we were in contact with. This went for the Germans— men, women, and children—the Frenchies, and the Uke maidens. Even the *Inspektor* was visibly impressed, and on a couple of occasions I heard him laying down the law to the Frenchies and holding us up as examples. Of course, we helped this era of goodwill along by doling out a few cigarettes where they would do the most good, and an occasional piece of chocolate to the tots cemented us with the womenfolk.

The Frenchies were a good lot, and their rations from the Pétain government were pitifully small. About once a month they were issued a sack of dried peas, a few biscuits, and a pack of really rugged French cigarettes. These were guaranteed to erode lung tissue in a week. The Frenchies had been extremely helpful to us in a number of ways. Aware of their plight, every once in a while we tried to give them a little coffee, cigarettes, or whatever we had to spare. Knowing how much the Germans and the Frenchies enjoyed a smoke, it is interesting to note that never to my knowledge did any of them ever ask for a cigarette.

The Poles were not so reticent. When we offered the pack around once in a while, they were always appreciative, though sometimes polite to the point of refusing. Of course we knew that this was carrying politeness too far. I do want to stress, however, that we were not indiscriminate in doling out cigarettes, as we had all learned long ago, in both Africa and Italy, that you lose esteem in the eyes of the natives if you are too generous. We had our little group of people whom we respected, and to these few we were generous.

One day about a week after our arrival, Franz Mahn was caught up with his chores, so I went out into the fields with Potato Pop and the main work detachment. With us this day was Johnny DiCrecchio, who normally worked with the woods crew. This, for both of us, was our maiden effort in the fields. Arriving at the target for the day, a turnip field, we joined with the Ukrainian girls, a few boys, and the ten or twelve teenaged German girls assigned to this job. We all had hoes and were to walk the length of the field between the rows of plants, hoeing out the weeds at the bases of the turnip plants both to the left and right of us. The field was at least six hundred feet long. We started in a long line from the near side. Johnny and I set about hoeing to the best of our ability, heads down, giving it the old college try. After about fifteen minutes, we heard roars of laughter up ahead and were embarrassed to see that while we had progressed about eighty feet, the rest of the line had gone almost three hundred feet. Old Potato Pops was disgusted as he dashed back to see what the hell was going on. Reaching us, he saw that Johnny was a lousy marksman and had mowed down as many young turnips as weeds. This really made him tear his hair out. Sending a couple of girls back to help us, he returned to the main group. For the rest of the day, Johnny and I each hoed single rows while the others had double row assignments. Even with this handicap, they showed us their heels every trip.

About a half hour after lunch, Johnny became acutely aware of his kidneys and cast his eye about for a good place to relieve himself. The land was as flat as an airstrip. The only cover in sight was a few rows of pines, planted as a windbreak, a half mile away. Johnny finally went to Potato Pop and explained his need. Pop, plainly exasperated at such a stupid request, shouted *"Ja, ja*, go, go," and swung his hand in an arc. Johnny, always polite, laid down his hoe and set off for the row of trees. Pop had his back to him, and it wasn't until he turned around a couple of minutes later that he realized where Johnny was headed for. By this time Johnny was a good hundred yards on his way and really making time. Pop let out a roar like a wounded buffalo: "Johann, where the hell do you think you're going? Isn't this field good enough for you to piss in? Perhaps you think you have some possession that the rest of us haven't?"

At this sally, the girls burst into roars of laughter and the guard was practically convulsed. Johnny, slowly returning, turned crimson. With an interested audience, he faced about and let her go. This incident tickled Pop and the guard, and they joked about it to Johnny for months.

The girls took a keen delight in the situation also, and before the day was over we could see why they thought Johnny's actions peculiar. Two or three of the *Mädchens* (girls) had similar problems later in the afternoon. With scant thought for propriety, they just squatted two or three feet out of the row so you wouldn't step on them, hoisted their skirts, and displaying a broad expanse of Teutonic buttock, let fly. Johnny was visibly agitated when this took place, and turnip mortality soared.

Benzin and *Herr Inspektor* had never heard of Walter Reuther and the eight-hour day. We worked from 6:00 A.M. to 5:00 P.M., with the teamsters leaving a half hour earlier and returning a half hour later because they had to feed, harness, and unharness their horses each day. We worked a full six-day week with Sunday off. Sunday was letter-writing day as well as sock-mending day, bath day, and laundry day.

With the *Inspektor*'s permission, we built a wooden bathtub on our first Sunday. It was 6 feet long, 30 inches wide, and 24 inches deep. After it was built, we coated it with a black tarlike substance that hardened and was waterproof. The bathtub was housed in the cattle barn, adjacent to the farmyard, where there was a large vat steam pressure cooker device where they prepared potatoes for the pigs. These were small potatoes, no good for any other purpose, which were fed into a massive hopper with a potato fork. The resulting mush was slopped up by the pigs with apparent relish. This boiler hookup guaranteed a constant supply of scalding water. One nice thing about having a black tub was that the ring didn't show.

The *Inspektor*'s house, the Ukrainian barracks, Franz Mahn's workshop, our barracks, and a couple of equipment sheds formed one side of the farmyard quadrangle. On the far side of the open space, parallel to these buildings, was the main barn, an extremely long brick, slate-roofed structure that quartered the horses, cows, oxen, and colts. Farm wagons and harnesses were also stored in the main barn. The upper story was used for storing sacked chemical fertilizers and seed potatoes.

The two short ends of the yard were fairly well blocked off by pigpens and smaller barns for hay and other crops. The open rectangular enclosure thus created was given over in part to an enormous dung heap. A good 12 feet deep, this pile was as large as the average city house lot. Cow manure, horse manure, chicken droppings—it was all hoarded. We were later to learn that this was the German barometer of wealth in the rural areas. Of course, when the wind was in the wrong direction things got a little ripe at the barracks. One thing was sure: we only had to sniff to know we were on a farm.

Another Sunday morning ritual was the emptying of the two-holer. This had a box inset that was removed from the side by a leather strap handle. Somehow we had scrounged a pair of canvas work gloves, and each Sunday a two-man detail removed the box, carried it to the dung heap, and returned the empty box for the next week's accumulation. I remember the Frenchies thought this was excruciatingly funny, and as we carted it past their front door they would all chorus "Tum, tum, ta, tum, da, da, tum," to the dirge of a funeral march.

One of our favorite recreations was pitching horseshoes. Horseshoes were plentiful at Benzin, and we picked up two short lengths of pipe from Franz Mahn. The Germans watched us pitching horseshoes with a great deal of interest, and as far as we could determine it was a pastime previously unknown in this part of Germany.

CHAPTER 8

The Affair of the Hen

Every Saturday night about eight o'clock the *Inspektor* would open our storeroom door, and we would bring in five Red Cross cartons for distribution. It was clear that I would have to go to Stolp in the near future, as our supply was getting low.

All of the parcels distributed from *Stalag* II B were American, though there were certain minor differences in content depending upon where they were packed. We soon learned these minor deviations covered options such as tuna fish instead of salmon, Spam instead of corned beef, etc. We all liked the American parcels, though there were two items that we envied from the other parcels: the tinned real butter in the Canadian parcel and the sweet condensed milk in the British.

After the first couple of weeks, our food preferences became known and trading on the *Stalag* basis was commonplace. I put quite an emphasis on converting other foodstuffs to prunes and was known as "Jack the Prune King." Jess McDonald developed a passion for seafood and was "Jess the Tuna King."

Several of the boys had been kidding Johnny DiCrecchio that the state of Maine did not contribute to our well-being because they provided no parcel food. They pointed to the origin of the Spam, salmon, biscuits, etc., to stress this fact. Then one night, as we opened parcels, Johnny let out a whoop of delight and went parading around the barracks proudly displaying a can of sardines from West Jonesport, Maine. The honor of the sovereign state of Maine thus redeemed, Johnny was smug for the rest of the month.

We had become especially friendly with three of the Frenchies. There was Camille, a small, gnomelike man with Eddie Cantor eyes and jug-handle ears, a mason by trade who was doing the same work at Benzin; Louis, an older man, who had been a teacher in a rural one-room schoolhouse in Brittany; and Gabrielle, who had a full set of gold teeth and a ferretlike face and affected a melodramatic black cape and wide-brimmed black hat.

Of the three, Louis was my favorite. He was a true friend, self-effacing, mild-mannered, and almost paternal. To his great embarrassment, I called him "Louis le Savant," to which he would go to great lengths to point out that he was only a humble teacher in a rural elementary school. He liked to come over on Sundays with his book of French arithmetic problems. Some of these involved simple algebraic equations set forth as problems, such as "If a man had four sons and their combined ages plus 35 equaled the age of the father," etc. He enjoyed working these puzzlers out with me and the others of our gang.

The most colorful of the Frenchies was Gabrielle, a lean Marseilles Frenchman with a glint in his eye and a mouthful of gold teeth that rivaled sunrise in the Bay of Naples. By his own account, his prewar existence had been a constant entangling in business deals of extremely dubious legality. He had lived by his wits, and there was no artifice in shrewd trading that he had not mastered. By his own admission he could outhaggle and outbargain any Arab in the Marseilles marketplace. Gabrielle had been a confirmed black marketer by the age of eight, and if someone hadn't derailed his career with an untimely knife thrust, he would probably now be either behind bars or among the business elite of Marseilles. He was quite a storyteller, with a true flair for the dramatic, and the other Frenchies roared as he told of his exploits along the waterfront and in the slum quarter of his native city.

Camille and Gabrielle were chess players, and they taught us a great deal about the game. Under their tutelage we became fair players, but never progressed to the point that we could give either of them much of a tussle.

We had brought a pack of playing cards out from the *Stalag*, and Sunday afternoons there was generally a good poker game. As at the *Stalag*, we posted exchange rates for parcel foods, the value expressed in terms of cigarettes. At one time, I thought the poker game stakes got a bit high and gave the boys a bit of a talking to. They took it in good spirits and agreed fully. That was the end of what might have become a serious problem. When you are living for a week out of the contents of a half-cubic-foot box, you realize that you can't afford to lose more than a token amount without creating hard feelings. The boys all saw the point, and although the card games continued from that time on, the stakes were more moderate. On the few other occasions when a policy of some kind had to be determined, I always found the boys reasonable and always had the unanimous backing of the group.

On Sundays, if the weather was at all pleasant, several Ukrainian and Polish boys would come over and chat with us through the fence. An unfortunate faux pas could have had serious repercussions one Sunday, but apparently no serious harm resulted. Our guard, who really had a nice setup with no duties of any consequence and lots of time to spend at the *Gasthaus*, was fairly talkative one Sunday and casually asked where I had been captured. Without too much thought, I answered "Anzio," adding that most of us had been taken in this area. Pausing a moment, he pointed to his eye socket and said *"Mein Auge—Anzio"* (my eye—Anzio). As soon as the words were out of my mouth, I knew from his expression that I had put my foot in the bucket, but there seemed no way to repair the damage. He remained silent for a minute or two, his good eye roaming over our crew and his mind no doubt pondering, *I wonder if it was one of these bastards that put my eye out.* You could have cut the silence with a knife. He then said, "Johann, what was your job in the army?" I certainly wasn't going to be caught in the same trap again and nonchalantly assured him that I had been a truck driver. He asked a few of the others, and not being slow on the uptake, they all knew enough to be cooks, mechanics, clerks, indeed anything unrelated to weapons.

Without pursuing the matter further, he turned abruptly and left for his afternoon stein of beer. We all felt uneasy for the next few days, but the subject was never again mentioned, and we did not seem to have worsened our position.

The Frenchman Gabrielle was a real businessman. He had some chore that made it necessary for him to work about the henhouse, and on some of his trips he would find a way of pirating an egg or two. At nine or nine-thirty at night, knowing our guard would not show up until ten, Gabrielle would sidle up to the fence, attract our attention with a few pebbles thrown against the door, and sell the egg for the going rate of six cigarettes. He never had any trouble finding customers. With his knee-length black cape, black broad-brimmed hat, and 14-karat bridgework, he looked like a character from some Lon Chaney melodrama. The mystery effect was further increased by his covert manner and whispered bargaining.

One night, Gabrielle almost got me into serious trouble. An ambitious man, he decided to go on from the egg business to bigger and better things—the poultry business. This was a risky undertaking, for had he been caught it would have gone hard with him. I heard the pebbles on the door and went out expecting to buy an egg, but I was floored when Gabrielle pulled back his cloak to reveal a chicken. First on the scene, I dickered and established a price of three packs of Camels, and the merchandise changed hands.

No sooner was I back in the barracks than I heard the crunch of gravel outside the door. It was our guard, a few minutes earlier than usual. I popped the chicken in an empty Red Cross box, not too perturbed because I knew the guard would be with us just long enough to count twenty heads and take a brief look about, no more than five minutes.

To my horror, just as the guard came in the door, the top of the Red Cross box began to jump up and down and faint noises came from the hen. Gabrielle, with true Gallic cunning, had only knocked the hen insensible, figuring no doubt that if he couldn't make a sale, he could always pop the hen back into the henhouse on his way home. I sat on the box, and the rest of the boys saved the day by laughing and talking in loud tones to distract the guard from my end of the room. The guard looked a bit puzzled, for we were generally a quiet bunch at 10:00 P.M., but it didn't arouse his suspicion and he soon left. After I heard his key in the door, the sound of receding footsteps, and the click of the outer gate padlock, I hauled out the hen and dispatched it for keeps. Shaken by this close call, I carefully plucked the hen and wrapped the feathers in paper, which one of the woods crew promised to bury the next day in the privacy of the forest.

Bill Walters, our cook, agreed to gut and boil the hen the next day. This was not much of a risk for Bill, as the guard was safely out of the way all day and no one else ever bothered to come to our barracks. Bill later told me that he was cautious nevertheless, closing the door during the cooking operation and keeping one eye on the path, remaining ready to duck the chicken, pot and all, under the nearest bed if anyone approached.

The chicken entrails and bones were temporarily lodged in the privy, and as I was on the emptying detail the next Sunday, I took care that any incriminating evidence was buried a good two feet deep in excrement.

Gabrielle showed up that Sunday afternoon, and I sure gave him hell. He got a big kick out of the story and pointed out that I shouldn't have assumed the bird was dead. All's well that ends well, however, and that chicken provided the tastiest meal I had enjoyed in many months.

By the end of our first month, everyone had pretty well settled down to the farm routine and we were an accepted part of the labor force. Except for Johnny and me and our fiasco with the hoeing, we had more than measured up to the *Inspektor*'s standards. The *Inspektor* never told us that, of course, but we heard it repeatedly from the Frenchmen and from Paul and Franz Mahn. Johnny and I were without doubt the world's worst hoers, but we held up our end of the bargain on any other jobs we were given. I never could fathom why we hated the hoe the way we did. It wasn't hard work. I guess it was just the fact that we were in a stooped-over position, or maybe we were like the potato sorter who had a nervous breakdown: "It wasn't the work; it was the constant decisions that had to be made."

Swede Olson was highly esteemed by the *Inspektor,* who put a lot of faith in his judgment. Conlin, Pierce, and Henderson were well-regarded teamsters who got the most out of their horses. They were complimented by their German counterparts for showing them some novel type of four- or six-horse hitch, which the Jerries first derided but later adopted themselves. Henderson and Conlin developed a sincere attachment to their horses and became quite upset at the miserable scanty rations given the animals. One day they openly belabored the *Inspektor* about it. Instead of blowing off steam, as we all expected him to, he actually backpedaled, conceded the animals were underfed, and slipped Conlin and Henderson a little more feed grain, unbeknownst to the German teamsters. Heinrich, the woods boss, had been known to say that his gang of Osak, McDonald, Benson, DiCrecchio, and Kudloski produced far more work than any of his former work groups of Frenchmen or Germans. This was high praise indeed.

I continued to alternate between Franz Mahn and Potato Pop, and at times I had a team of oxen to drive. The oxen did not respond to any spoken commands, so ox team pilots made their desires known by use of a wooden club much like a baseball bat. The oxen were seldom yoked and when working had a harness rigged up so they were actually pulling with their foreheads. This was the subject of a running controversy between the Germans and our own farm experts—Henderson, Halvorsen, Olson, et al.—who contended that oxen pulled far more effectually with their shoulders and necks rather than with the tops of their skulls. Similarly, there was not a horse collar on the farm. The horses all worked from a breast harness, and here once again there was a marked difference of opinion.

For three days I was on a fence-building project with Franz Mahn. They were laying out a pasture, or exercise yard, for a few young colts, so we put up a barbed wire–enclosed yard leading off from the rear barn door. We had a posthole digger and it was good digging, light soil and virtually no rocks. The poles up, we rolled out large coils of wire and stapled the wire to the posts, first drawing the wire taut with a chain and clamp device.

One week, I was sent down to help old Gustave Topel, the blacksmith. He was a fine old man, and I liked working with him in the little one-room shop. My primary duties were to work the bellows and sharpen axes. One day, old Gustave had me hold while he struck with a sledge. I was fearful for my knuckles and I guess my face showed it, for old Gus laughed and said, "What are you worried about, Johann? I've done this all my life and haven't hit anyone yet." To demonstrate his good faith, he even held for a spell while I struck with the sledge. He really had a lot of trust. I still remember the acrid smell of the metal in the forge and the salt crystals that were thrown on the flickering flames, making them glow in a brilliant range of colors. Sometimes we had horses to shoe, another assignment I didn't relish.

Our little blacksmith shop was on the one road that bisected Benzin, indeed the only surfaced road in town. It was not asphalt but cobbled, and the entire village was strung out along this artery like a crooked shoestring. Most of the passersby were on foot or cycling, though once or twice a day there might be a motorcycle or a truck. The village women brought us their pots and pans for mending and knives, scissors, and scythes for sharpening. All metal was hoarded. Tiny children often brought in horseshoe nails picked up from the road and were rewarded with a pat on the head and a few words of commendation from old Gus.

Stocks of parts for agricultural equipment were nonexistent in Benzin and the surrounding region, so Franz Mahn often brought down crude sketches or sample parts to be duplicated to keep the harrows, mowers, and other equipment operative. It was amazing how some stopgap contraption could be contrived to hold the rig together for a while longer.

In my work with Franz Mahn, I formed a high opinion of his capabilities. He had acute limitations as far as world events, literature, or the classics were concerned, but in the manual arts he was a wizard. In addition to general maintenance chores, he doubled as the farm veterinarian, wound armatures, designed emergency replacement mechanical parts, and knew no limitations in carpentry or design. He was quite a fellow.

I was next used to tend the masons, and have often thought that a wanted criminal could do this job to eradicate his finger-prints. At times I thought my fingers were worn down to the first joint. Camille and an old German, Max, were the two regu-lar masons on the farm, and the *Inspektor* had ordered work to be started on a major addition to the big barn. My job was to mix cement for both bricklayers, and also to see that they were always well supplied with bricks. This was a real backbreaker. The equipment consisted of a wooden box about six feet by eight feet to mix the cement in and a hoe for "puddling." The worst part of the job was puddling with the hoe, by no means my favorite tool, to ensure a thorough mixture. The recipe was forty shovels of sand, twelve shovels of cement, add water to right consistency, and then hoe like hell. Each batch had to be pushed around a good half hour before it was ready to use. After a batch had been made, I dashed about for the next half hour, piling up bricks next to each of the bricklayers. When I was about to drop from hustling about with armloads of bricks, I would see that my boys had made deep inroads into my mor-tar supply, so I'd hurry back to mix up a fresh batch. I heartily disliked this assignment. I would hit the sack about 8:00 P.M. to be ready for the next grueling day.

After three days on mason-tending duty, the *Inspektor* stopped me one night on my way back to the barracks. He told me he had to send a wagon into Stolp the next morning and wanted me to go along to assist in the unloading. He added that the Red Cross parcels were getting low and that I could replen-ish the stock in the same trip. This was certainly welcome news, for in addition to a great deal of excitement and anticipation about visiting Stolp and meeting Jack Schick, I was extremely pleased to get away from the damned cement and brick for a day. The brick wall was inching higher almost imperceptibly, yet I felt as if I had already helped build the Great Wall of China.

That night, I made lists of the various articles I would try to obtain and a list of all the boys' shirt and shoe sizes. Everyone had a thousand suggestions. Finally Swede Olson got a little weary of the chatter and made one of his infrequent pronouncements: "Jack will get as much and as good a lot of supplies as he can. Let's all shut up and tomorrow night by this time we'll know how he made out."

CHAPTER 9

A Visit to Stolp

Seven o'clock the next morning, Hans, the young lad who had met us on our arrival at Benzin, pulled up in front of the barracks with the team and wagon. The guard was already aboard. Commandeering Bill Walters for half an hour, we drove over to one of the barns and piled on a good load of sacked rye. It was a beautiful June morning, and knowing I had at least a three-hour ride ahead, I lay back on the grain sacks for a relaxing look at the countryside, then at its peak of beauty. The road wound along, cobbled all the way, through great stands of pine, then into open fields and meadows. The road was flanked for miles with vast fields green with tender young shoots of grain fresh broken through the brown soil. Every half mile or so, we would pass a cottage with a conventional vegetable patch in the rear and flower garden in the front, where we would expect a lawn in America. These were all brick structures, some with slate roofs, the humbler ones thatched. It was striking how few people seemed to be about. The sun climbed in a great parabola of vibrant warmth, and there was little noise except a constant creaking of wagon wheels over cobbles against a backdrop of plodding hoof beats. There was a dearth of conversation, as both Hans and the guard seemed content to let nature hold center stage.

After we had gone about five miles, the road crossed a double set of railroad tracks and, for the next two miles, paralleled a military airfield. We knew there was an airfield in the immediate area because training planes often flew overhead as we labored in the fields, looping and flying in formation. A tall

anchor-wire fence bordered the airfield up to the point where
our tributary road joined a major roadway. Turning to the
right, we now passed the front of the airfield with several large
hangars and numerous single-story personnel barracks for the
Luftwaffe (air force) flyers and ground crew. The barracks were
rather attractive, with gay gardens clustered about a semicircu-
lar driveway leading up to the administration building, obvious
by its flagpole and sentries.

On this main road, traffic picked up. There was quite a
lot of horse-drawn traffic, mostly farm carts bringing produce
into the Stolp market, and a few trucks. The trucks were as odd
a lot of Rube Goldberg mechanical devices as I had ever seen.
They burned a variety of fuels, including charcoal, diesel oil,
and even soft coal. Tire treads were uniformly bald, and I'm
willing to bet the tubes had patches on top of patches. Their
best days were way behind them. Wheezing along, it looked no
better than even money they would make it to Stolp without a
breakdown.

We were now going down the long cobbled incline into
Stolp proper. The open fields gave way to city streets and
blocks of apartments and warehouse buildings. How odd to see
streetcars again. Atop one of the buildings was an advertising
sign bearing a picture of a well-known bottle and the legend
TRINK COCA-COLA. Around a bend in the road, I saw my first
German gas station. The familiar Shell sign looked utterly out
of place here.

We had entered Stolp from its seamier side, but though we
were in the warehouse, soft coal, and low-rent district, I could
see glimpses of more sedate avenues paralleling ours a few
blocks removed. The wagon abruptly turned into a narrow
alley, and after Hans spent ten minutes finding the proper
address, we unloaded our rye.

After the first few sacks were off, the guard called to Hans
and pointed out that we could all make better use of our time
if he and I went on to the Red Cross center while Hans and the
others finished unloading the wagon. Hans readily agreed, as
there was plenty of help available and the goods for the return

trip were to be loaded at still another warehouse. It seemed the Red Cross Center was a well-known place, for Hans didn't ask for any directions where to pick us up.

The guard and I set off on foot. The first few blocks were in a mixed tenement and warehouse district of Stolp, but in a few minutes we turned onto a wide, tree-lined boulevard with a park on one side. This was early afternoon on an ideal June day, and the park benches were well occupied by well-dressed people. After so many months of seeing only uniforms and rustic farm clothes, I had almost forgotten that there were such things as tailored suits and dresses. Many of the younger women in the park were governesses or nursemaids with two or three youngsters in tow.

As we got into the business and shopping area, it was plain to see that although the storefronts were impressive, there weren't many luxury items on sale. The display windows were virtually empty, and the clerks outnumbered the cash customers. Air raid sirens were mounted prominently on rooftops and street-corner poles, and large painted arrow signs indicated the nearest air raid shelters.

In another few minutes we were at our destination. A group of massive buildings bordered three sides of a large field, the entire area equaling four normal-sized city blocks. This was the Stolp *Kaserne,* a sort of armory and officer's training school combined. A five-story brownstone building, with its flagstaffs and array of command cars parked in the courtyard, appeared to be the military headquarters for the entire Stolp area. The guard told me that before World War I, this had been the training grounds and headquarters of a crack cavalry outfit, Von Mackenson's Death's Head Hussars, and the expanse of turf had been the scene of precision cavalry maneuvers and polo games. There was a sort of nostalgia in the way he told of the advent of the panzer divisions that relegated the dashing cavalrymen forever to the history books.

Just inside the door of the cavernous main building were pictures of Von Mackenson and glass cases filled with plaques, lances, battle standards, and official commendations given to detachments for accomplishments on the field of battle. I found out later that Von Mackenson had been a native son of Stolp, and the town parks and public squares boasted many statues of the local celebrity.

Although the long line of stables just on the far side of the drill field was still in good repair, they were now used for parking trucks and housing vehicle repair depots. The German army still depended heavily on horseflesh, but now the emphasis was on draft animals like Percherons. Fleet ponies no longer had any place in modern warfare.

The *Kaserne* was enormous. As my boots echoed hollowly down miles of cavernous brownstone corridors, I could not help but liken the building to a vast fortress. Now that the war was in full swing, this group of buildings housed a regiment of reserve troops, a company or two of SS troopers, and some convalescing soldiers. Much of the floor space was devoted to recordkeeping, with vast rooms packed with tiers of filing cabinets. From certain cryptic remarks dropped by Hans (who was fifteen and slated for the *Wehrmacht* before he got much older), I gathered this was also the headquarters of the German version of a draft board. When we were in the fields, far from other ears, Hans—a bright boy and well-liked by all of our crew at Benzin—had made it clear to us that he had little desire for a military career.

The complex also housed at least 2,000 French and Belgian prisoners. These prisoners worked in factories, railroad yards, and other places of employment where there were no provisions for housing. There was no such thing as an industrial deferment in Germany during the years 1942 through 1945, and in consequence there were thousands of small business establishments where practically all the male tradesmen were off doing their bit for the Fatherland. These businesses were now operated essentially by French forced labor, with the family patriarch brought out of retirement to supervise the operations. These forced laborers had few restrictions to contend with, at least as far as freedom of movement was concerned, and were a familiar sight in the Stolp streets. These "trusties" were to be found in warehouses, behind the counters in butcher shops, in garages, and engaged in the building trades.

A few of them hinted to me, with a true Gallic glint, that they kept the home fires burning in more ways than one, and that many a *Frau* would be sorely disappointed when—and if— her warrior husband came home. This may have been so in a few cases, but I feel the vast majority of these contentions were the workings of overactive imaginations and a desire to impress the American that they were true boudoir Frenchmen. From the appearance of many of these self-proclaimed lotharios, if what they claimed was indeed true, the *Fraus* must have been in really desperate straits.

Way down in the subbasement was a fair-sized room bearing a neatly lettered sign: AMERICAN RED CROSS. After leading me to the door, the guard consulted his watch and announced he would be back in an hour.

Jack Schick was alone in the room. A slight, dark-haired fellow from Chicago, he introduced himself and inquired how we were making out at Benzin. He briefly explained that his area was a rough circle extending about fourteen miles from the hub, Stolp. For almost a thousand American prisoners in this district, he was the link with the *Stalag*, and in extreme cases with Geneva. Schick seemed a pleasant, competent administrator, and from his questions appeared to be keenly interested in our experience at Benzin.

Schick indicated that we could have a month's supply of food parcels (twenty cases, four cartons per man) and a limited amount of clothing. From my list of sizes, I was able to pick up six shirts, five pairs of shoes, five pants, and two combat suits. We also received a stock of razor blades, an assortment of underwear, twelve pairs of socks, several knitted wool hats, an overcoat, several books, and a softball and bat.

At this time, and on all subsequent visits, I found Schick to be a sincere, efficient person, always ready to see that all of the boys in his area got a fair share of whatever he could muster up from his dispersal point. He wanted a report on our doings at Benzin, and I truthfully told him that we were reasonably well treated and had no great kick at the moment. While we were chatting, one or two other GIs came in from other *Kommandos*, and Jack took care of their requirements as best he could.

I soon found out that Jack Schick was the fountainhead of all GI news. He briefed us on the current situation on the Russian and Italian fronts and reported the widespread belief that a massive assault on the French coast was imminent. Schick's sources were reliable Poles and Frenchmen who gleaned their data from BBC broadcasts. If a few Red Cross cigarettes were expended in this news gathering, it was a case of commodities well spent. The opportunity to go back to the farm with factual good news was a tremendous morale factor, not only for us but for all the rest of the GIs in and around Stolp. The news about recent devastating Allied air strikes in major cities of western Germany was particularly heartening.

All too soon, Hans and the guard appeared in the doorway. Schick gave a couple of Frenchies a few cigarettes to help Hans and me lug the parcels and other supplies through the maze of corridors and out to the wagon, which was drawn up in the drill field. This had been an epic day. I couldn't wait to get back to the barracks to distribute the parcels and clothing and to impart my war news to just about the most appreciative audience a man could have.

But the surprises were not at an end. About halfway home, we approached a *Gasthaus*, and the guard told Hans to pull into the paved inn yard. This was no great shock, for we all knew that old "Squinty" was no teetotaler. What did rock me was when he turned in his seat and said, "Would you like a beer, Johann?" Even Hans's eyebrows went up at that, and still more so when he was included in the invitation. We both took him up on the offer with alacrity. I was going to have trouble peddling this story at Benzin, I knew.

Entering the tavern, I took pains to take a seat where I could keep my eye on the wagon full of Red Cross parcels parked outside. Both Hans and the guard were quite amused at this and commended me on my vigilance.

It was cool and dim in the tavern, and the pungent smell of malt and hops permeated the very rafters. We were the only customers at the moment. Behind the bar, a small table radio blared out some brassy marching songs, presumably calculated to rouse patriotic German hearts, but from all outward signs it missed its mark with my two companions.

No sooner were we seated at the table than the barmaid was there for our orders. This was the high point of the day. She had more curves than a scenic railway. About twenty-five, she was of generous proportions cast in the ever-popular Brunnhilde mold. Alongside this bar wench, Margie Hart [a popular 1940s pinup] was an anemic stripling. As she leaned over, rag in hand, to sweep off our already immaculate table, I nearly felt dizzy observing that snowy vista. From a morale point of view, this vision beat martial music all to hell.

As soon as she brought over three man-sized tankards, Hans and Squinty began to josh me about my reaction, which must have been pretty obvious. The beer hit the spot and was very refreshing. Once the beer was gone, Squinty let forth with a monumental belch and, glancing at his watch, let us know it was high time to hit the Benzin trail. Going out the door, I caught my last fleeting glimpse of the barmaid, still wiping vigorously at some nonexistent stain while I tried to gauge her impact on the next customer.

We pulled into the farmyard about seven o'clock. After the guard got the storeroom key from the *Inspektor*, lots of the boys turned out to stack our new Red Cross parcels. Inside the barracks, I piled up the clothing and distributed it to the boys who needed it the most. In one or two instances where a choice was difficult, they drew straws. We were not too badly off for clothing, and the distribution seemed to meet with everyone's approval. For a good twenty minutes, I rattled off my second-hand BBC war communiqués to an enraptured audience. The books went like hotcakes, but the big hit of the trip seemed to be the softball and bat.

CHAPTER 10

The Woods Crew

A day or so after my junket to Stolp, Squinty told us he was being replaced in a week. It appeared that he had been given the news when reporting to his superiors at the *Kaserne* while I was downstairs talking with Schick and stocking up on supplies. This spelled the Russian front, and it must have been a rude awakening to Squinty, who had pretty soft duty at Benzin with a private room, no duties to speak of, ample beer, and no doubt all of the evening assignments he could handle with the frustrated *Fräuleins* of Benzin. No wonder his mood had been unpredictable on the return wagon ride from Stolp. I commiserated as best as I could, and with a grin and a return of his *Gasthaus* attitude, he shrugged. *"Das ist der Krieg"* (That's war). All in all, he had not been a bad sort and we looked on his leaving with some misgivings. We had gone from the frying pan into the fire often enough to be wary of changes.

By now all of us GIs spoke creditable German, even if our sentence structure left something to be desired. We were an accepted part of the local scene. About this time, I got away from my odd-job assignments and became a regular member of the woods crew. This was a welcome change, for I honestly enjoyed the work, laborious as it was. Each morning our five-man crew would take off with Heinrich, the woods boss, stop at the smithy to put an edge on our axes, and go felling Norway pine. It was healthful, invigorating work, and as time passed we became so proficient at timber felling that Heinrich's supervision was almost cursory.

The forest stretched for miles, all hand-planted pine in perfect rows. One could look down the limitless corridors for vast distances. As each tree was the same precise distance from its neighbor, the forest gave the uniformly ruled appearance of a sheet of graph paper. There was a complete absence of underbrush, and the carpet of pine needles underfoot was inches thick.

Each timber section bore a sign giving the year of planting, and at five-year intervals these areas were thinned 50 percent. Overhead was a roof of green, and even on rainy or snowy days very little penetrated this ceiling of foliage. Each tree, the precise replica of its neighbor, would have made a mast for a sailing vessel. Each trunk grew straight up, with not a branch for fifty or sixty feet, then a dense green tuft for the final third of its height. The only minor defect to some trees—and this infuriated Heinrich—were occasional healed-over small scars about three feet from the ground. Heinrich explained that this damaged was inflicted by deer that at certain times of the year, when they were acquiring new antlers, rubbed the embryo horns on the boles of the trees. It was common to see deer in the forest, and their droppings and trails were in evidence in every direction.

Heinrich would identify the work area for the day and go ahead with a hand hatchet, blazing the trees to be felled. I came along next to notch each blazed tree two or three inches above ground level in the direction that it was to fall. Two saw teams of two men each followed. Kneeling on each side of the tree, posteriors pointing the way it would fall and knuckles rubbing the ground, they sawed through to about a half inch from the notch. Sliding out the saw, they then gave the tree a shove with the axe, and down it would crash.

We became so expert in this that we could drop them on a dime—or in Pomerania, a *Pfennig*. Once in a while a falling tree would hang up on another tree. Then we would drop still another tree in such a manner that both trees would be freed and fall. Once in a while, a tree would kick back from the stump as it started on its final crash. This called for some lively footwork by the saw team. Heinrich and I would finish our chores in a couple of hours, then come back to form a third sawing team.

After the midday lunch break, we halted the felling and set in lopping off the branches of the felled trees and sawing off the thin terminal ends. The next step was to pick up the trees, one man to each end, hoist them on our shoulders, and pile them up next to the woods road to be loaded on wagons and carted to the sawmill. The first week both my shoulders were like raw hamburger at the end of the day. We soon became hardened to it and thought nothing of two of us walking off with a 40-foot log 15 inches in diameter at the butt and tapering to about 6 inches at the thin end.

Very often the last hour of work was given over to chopping and stacking cordwood. Four sharpened branches were pounded into the ground with the flat of an axe, creating an enclosure. The decent-sized branches were chopped into 24-inch lengths and stacked inside the retaining poles.

In the mornings, as we strode off to the woods, the village women and children were out in full force attending to a variety of chores. No one idled in Benzin, not in wartime at any rate. It was a common sight to see old grandmothers filling water pails at their outdoor hand pumps. First a little priming, then some vigorous pulls at the 8-foot sweep handles would get the water surging out of the spout. When two buckets were filled, they were suspended on a shoulder yoke and carried into the houses. The children each had their own little flock of geese, which were marched down to the pond every morning in a dignified single-file procession. The young boys took this assignment very seriously indeed and maintained order among their charges with little string whips.

There was much amusement one morning when a gander took a violent dislike to DiCrecchio and, wings flapping and hissing for all it was worth, went onto the attack. The goose went after Johnny in a very vulnerable region, and for a couple of moments it looked as if Johnny might be fated to go through life a eunuch. Heinrich, in particular, got a big kick out of this incident.

Our primary job was felling timber, but occasionally the routine would be varied and we would spend a day snaking out some of the very large felled logs alongside the woods road. For this purpose, we had an exceptionally well-trained pair of horses who knew just when to lunge and when they could slack up. Once the log picked up impetus, we helped matters along by laying down small roller logs to reduce the friction. Once we used a team of oxen for this work, but they were not as satisfactory as the horses.

Normally we worked on Norway pine from 12 inches to 15 inches at the butt. One week we had quite a departure from routine when we cut down some mammoth black beech with a gasoline saw, and then split the 4-foot sawed sections with wedges and a sledge. There were some sections that split with virtually no trouble, but on every tree there was always one bastardly section, about fifteen feet up from the base, where four or five major limbs all took off in divergent directions. Splitting these sections was fiendish. At times we would have as many as eight wedges embedded before we broke through. Sometimes a few girls went along with us and peeled the bark from the felled trees with a sort of wood chisel blade on the end of a hoe handle.

It was impressive how every part of the tree was put to some practical use. There was absolutely no waste. We cut them down flush with the ground, and then trimmed off the few branches at the tip. The log was left in one piece down to the point where its diameter dropped to 6 inches. From this point on, the rest was cut in short lengths and piled as cordwood. There was even a small girl who carted off baskets full of sawdust. We strongly suspected that the sawdust was the basic ingredient of the weekly bread ration, but could never prove it.

Toward noon, Heinrich would pull out a saucer-sized pocket watch and announce it was lunchtime. We generally took about thirty to forty minutes, plenty of time for our one sandwich, a leisurely cigarette, and a measure of conversation or reflection. Flat on our backs, the air redolent with resin, gazing up through the pine tops to an azure sky, our thoughts would wander. About six o'clock, with the sun well above the horizon, the watch would be produced again and Heinrich would call it quits for the day. The axes and wedges would be covered over with pine boughs, and we would tramp through Benzin back to the barracks.

Benzin was quite a pretty place in many ways, a cluster of neat brick houses, most with thatched roofs. Each house boasted its own little vegetable plot in the rear, and in true European style a flowerbed in the front yard. The people were essentially straightforward and as provincial a group as I had ever met. Any villager who had been as far as Danzig was regarded as a world traveler. Most families had a son or two in military service, and like parents the world over were very concerned over their welfare. Many houses in town had already received news of the loss of a loved one.

One old soul had a boy who was a prisoner of the Allies, and several times she asked me if I was certain that he was being well treated. I assured her that he was no doubt well looked after, and this seemed to encourage her. She repeatedly wanted to know all about the climate and other data about Otava, where he was being held. Otava didn't ring a bell with me, not in the U.S. where she insisted he was, so I surmised it was some whistle-stop in the Plains states. She persisted that it was quite a large city, and with equal vehemence I assured her that it couldn't be. Finally, in desperation at my apparent ignorance, she wrote the word on a piece of paper and showed it to me. Looking at the paper, the whole matter became clear and I roared with laughter, the woman staring at me as if I had surely gone daft. The boy was in Ottawa, Canada, and as in the German tongue the "W" is given the "V" sound, the word had been so altered in pronunciation I hadn't been able to identify the place. I painted a glowing picture of the kindnesses of the Canadians and told her that Ottawa was just about on the same parallel of latitude as Benzin, with comparable seasons and climate.

There were no autos in Benzin. Grandmothers, old men, tots, and even *Herr Inspektor* were accomplished cyclists and pedaled about the village. The German girls with whom we worked were friendly, though in a reserved way, and all seemed to answer to Ilsa, Herta, or Hetwig. Benzin parents had little flair for originality where names were concerned. The girls were no raving beauties, but then we certainly saw them under the most adverse conditions. Cosmetics and makeup had no place in Benzin life, and their working outfits were men's pants or long shapeless skirts topped with a drab work shirt. Their hair was concealed by shawls or turbans, and it is hard to display a shapely ankle in a pair of wooden clogs.

Once in a great while, a soldier would come home for a short visit, and the girls would all be whispering and giggling like mad throughout his furlough. I have no doubt that the returning warrior was more worn out when he quitted Benzin than when he arrived. If he wasn't, it certainly was not the fault of the frustrated *Fräuleins* of Benzin. Of course, these were all farm girls, and the birds and the bees was old news to them, just by observation, by the time they were ten. They enjoyed a certain amount of coarse humor, which we were not loath to provide. They wouldn't have understood subtlety.

There was a patch of woodland along the path to the timber lots where a peculiar white fungus flourished. These were some variation of mushroom shaped in the image of a phallus. Passing this spot one day, we heard the girls whispering and snickering, and DiCrecchio brought the house down by asking them why they didn't bury the dead a little deeper. They considered this a hilarious sally.

We got so confused with the similarity of Christian names that we made up our own nicknames for them. Needless to say the names were not especially flattering, a few being "Five by Five," "the Monster," and "Meatball." They were all hard workers brought up in the tradition of the twelve-hour day, and they showed a great amount of respect to their parents. The mother or father had only to speak or frown to secure instant compliance. It appeared the Benzinians gave more than lip service to the old axiom about sparing the rod and spoiling the child.

The girls' big entertainment came when the prize village bull was put through his paces on a studding assignment. They would ring the barbed-wire fence during the performance, shrieking with vicarious amusement.

The only village siren was the postmistress, a very aloof girl who had been to Berlin and didn't condescend to mix with the rest of the *Mädchens*. She was reasonably attractive and once in a while would give the Benzin oldsters something to ogle at by wearing a pair of abbreviated shorts. Her pretensions of grandeur had made her persona non grata with the other girls, and there were no eligible males in the right age bracket or social status to take up the slack. She must have led a rather lonely existence.

There were two young lads in the village whom we came to know well. Young Hans was the bright friendly boy of fifteen who was due almost any month to be called to the colors. The other boy we had frequent contact with was Helmut, a comical figure with a perpetual grin and eyes so crossed you got dizzy just looking at him. Helmut was short a few buttons, but many of us GIs thought he added on a bit for good measure. One day when he and I were alone, he grinned and, pointing to his head in comical fashion, said "My poor head is not good enough for the *Wehrmacht.*" I swear one lid then drooped in a mammoth wink. Perhaps Helmut had more of his buttons than any of his village acquaintances gave him credit for.

In early June there were two personnel changes at the barracks. Walters went out into the fields, and Delbert Kinder became our cook. This was an amicable swap of jobs, as Kinder's soup was no better than Walters's was. Also, Elmer Eagle joined the teamsters, so we now had five full-time wagon jockeys.

Elmer was quite a boy. He hailed from a little spot in West Virginia called by the unlikely name of Droop. This earned for him the sobriquet of "The Drip from Droop." He was quite young, though stocky, and boasted a flowing Howard Taft–model mustache. Prior to joining the army, he had led a very provincial existence, and he kept most of us in stitches with his naive accounts of life in Droop. Saturday night was the highlight of the week, when he went across the valley to his uncle's house to listen to the radio. He went to great lengths to let us know that he was fairly well off financially, often stating that back home in Droop he had a snuffbox "'most full of dimes." This was a guaranteed mirth provoker, though Elmer couldn't quite see what there was to laugh about.

CHAPTER 11

The Arrival of Uncle Ben

As expected, one day Squinty was missing and a new guard became our keeper. This was a kindly white-haired man of about sixty-five who had been a librarian. There was absolutely no malice in him, and he was almost apologetic when he aroused us in the mornings. He was soon dubbed "Uncle Ben." The *Wehrmacht* was scraping the bottom of the manpower barrel for sure.

On the first day of his arrival, as I engaged him in conversation inside the barracks, Osak removed the firing pin from Ben's rifle, which Ben had left leaning against the wall. I'm sure he never missed the firing pin, for I'm sure he never cleaned the rifle. He was a real gentleman, polite almost to the point of being courtly, and with just a trace of the schoolmaster about him. He was sincerely sorry for us, frequently inquired about our parents, and hoped that the war would soon be over so we could return to our kinfolk. This was the last thing we had expected, an idealistic pacifist in *Wehrmacht* gray.

Old Ben was a real prince. He was very fond of all children and always had a kindly pat on the head for the village kiddies as we passed through Benzin proper on our way to the fields. If there had been a couple of million like him in Germany in 1938, Corporal Hitler would never have gotten his schemes off the ground.

As May gave way to June and then July, the days lengthened tremendously, and so did our working hours. In mid-July it was light enough to read a newspaper outdoors at 10:00 P.M. with no difficulty. I could never quite understand this, as by my reckoning we were no farther north than Montreal, yet we were getting conditions that should have prevailed much closer to the Pole. Perhaps the answer was that the Germans had screwed up the clock and had gone into some double Daylight Saving system. We were now into the most arduous part of the farming cycle and frequently labored in the fields and woods until 8:00 P.M.

One day in the woods, we were carrying out some very heavy logs. They were 50-footers, about fifteen inches at the butt and heavy as only green lumber can be. These larger logs required three men, one at each end and one in the middle, to get the log up on our shoulders and walk it over to the roadside about three hundred feet away. Johnny DiCrecchio was a good 8 inches shorter than either Jess McDonald or me, and he thought it a huge joke to be the man in the middle with the log riding well off his shoulder and borne entirely by the two end men. DiCrecchio made the mistake of ribbing Jess and me about this, and we decided to fix his wagon. On the next trip, Jess was the lead man and we let Johnny take the middle station without protest. Jess took a slightly different course that brought us up over a little knoll. When middle man DiCrecchio reached the crest of the little hillock, he took the full brunt of the weight. It damn near killed him. Of course, Jess and I knew what was going to happen, and when Johnny crumpled, we took the impact. Had we each stepped clear at the moment when Johnny got the whole load, he would have been seriously hurt. It threw quite a scare into him, and DiCrecchio was a chastened man the rest of the day. Old Heinrich had been observing us and he got a real chuckle out of the incident. It was poetic justice with a vengeance. Johnny carried his full share of the load from that time on.

On my trip to Red Cross headquarters in Stolp, I had been given a packet of vegetable seeds, which we entrusted to cook Walters to plant and nourish. Whether or not Walters forgot to water them we never knew, but nothing came of our gardening efforts except a few marble-sized radishes. We really needed the vegetables in our diet. By mid-June, at least half our crew of GIs was afflicted with boils. They seemed to center on either the feet or ankles, or else on the back of the neck. I had quite a crop on my neck. This was a common complaint shared by GI and civilian alike and came from the heavy concentration of starch in our diets. Potatoes, potatoes, potatoes, three times a day. On a subsequent trip to the *Lazarette* at Stolp with Hank Conlin, I was given a jar of ichthyol ointment by the doctor there, which helped some. Those boils were damn painful and left indentations like nail holes when they finally passed away.

Commencing at *Stalag* VII A in Moosburg, we had all been permitted to mail one postcard and one letter a week. I sometimes sent an extra letter or two, as some of the boys didn't write regularly. The first two weeks at Benzin had been murder, for we were quite weak and entirely unaccustomed to long hours of heavy manual labor. During this period, we all turned in to bed shortly after finishing our evening meal. We rapidly became accustomed to the hard work, and soon we all enjoyed a couple of hours' conversation in the barracks after supper. Lights out was at 10:00 P.M., and the heavy wooden shutters for our two windows had to be firmly in position before our single light could be turned on. When we arrived we'd had just the one tiny bulb that lit only the center of the room, leaving the corners in semidarkness. After we had been there a few weeks, particularly after my initial trip to Stolp when I brought back some good reading matter, I asked the *Inspektor* for a better bulb. He carried on in the worst way but finally relented and gave us a bulb that provided considerably more illumination.

It was the *Inspektor*'s habit to go into a tantrum at the simplest request. This was true not only of his dealings with us, but also with the villagers, the Frenchies, the Ukes, and his wife. He was an awesome sight, roaring away at the top of his voice, face beet red, pounding his fist into his palm. The villagers were frankly afraid of him, and he made capital of the fact. It had become second nature with him. Indeed, I think if any bystander on a Stolp street had asked him for a match, he would have gone into the same routine.

After the first few weeks, we all got into the habit of staying up until 10:00 P.M. Of course, in midsummer we frequently worked until 7:30 P.M. or later, and during the harvest season until 8:00 P.M., so that still didn't make for much spare time after we had downed the soup of the day supplemented by some parcel fare. Generally three or four boys would start a card game, others would read or write letters home, and the rest would stretch out on their bunks and exchange gossip of the day's happenings in their respective work groups. Some of the boys would darn socks or do simple sewing repairs. Kinder and Pierce were fair barbers, by Benzin standards at any rate, and they cut our hair in the evenings.

Sunday was bath day, and after cleaning up, we would all deck ourselves out in our best uniforms and march down to the village *Sportplatz*, or athletic field, about a half mile from our barracks, for the weekly softball game. This always drew a few spectators who never did quite fathom what the game was all about but got a kick out of it nevertheless. Sunday evenings we generally had a few Poles and Ukrainians come over from adjacent farms to see our Uke neighbors. One of the boys, a redheaded Pole, invariably brought his accordion and reeled off polkas and mazurkas while the rest sang folksongs or danced in the farmyard with the Ukes. Most of these Poles had quite a measure of freedom and could go about as they pleased on their day off.

Along with the youngsters, a couple of older men always came by, primarily for a couple of free cigarettes. With elaborate caution, guaranteed to arouse the suspicions of anyone in sight, they would whisper through the fence in Polish or Slovak to Kudloski, Osak, or Estock, who would relay the news on to the rest of us. The news always told of smashing Russian victories but was vague geographically, with no place names provided. I frankly took much of this with a large grain of salt, but later found from other sources, primarily Jack Schick, that it was essentially true, albeit embellished, as any good story is.

The reasons these forced laborers were not guarded were probably twofold. First, German military manpower was vitally needed for the much more important tasks at hand, and secondly, these personnel were not captured military but merely relocated farm workers, many of whose allegiance might have been dubious in the first place. There were one or two exceptions to this rule. One was a Polish captain who had been taken in the first few weeks of the war during the bloody siege of Westerplatte Island in Danzig Harbor, when the heroic garrison there was decimated. This fellow was an entirely different type of person from the rest of the rustics, by his bearing and demeanor a man of knowledge and culture. I placed a lot of reliability in his reports, which were always much more specific than those of his countrymen. How strange it was to realize that we were at almost the precise geographical location at which the war had started. Stolp had been one of the marshaling points for the *Blitzkrieg* unleashed against the Danzig corridor back in 1939. We had come full circle. Among other reports given us by the former Polish captain was word of the abortive attempt on Hitler's life on July 20, 1944. He had the news shortly after it occurred and long before the Western world knew of it.

It was during such a Sunday evening in June in the pastoral surroundings of Benzin that my "romance" blossomed. This was hatched and fostered by Jim Osak and was one of those cases where an interpreter went overboard with malice aforethought. There was a girl called Kvania who was one of the regular Sunday visitors. She was about six foot two inches in stocking feet and built on the general lines of a well-filled silo. I would have put my money on Kvania in a two-out-of-three fall match with Jim Londos [a Depression-era professional wrestler].

For all of her imposing physique, Kvania had a pleasant face and a naive, childlike simplicity. One evening, I saw Osak whispering through the fence to her and glancing and repeatedly pointing in my direction. God knows what wild yarn he may have told her. I didn't pay much attention until about fifteen minutes later, when she came up to the fence near me and shyly handed me a bunch of wildflowers that she had gone off and picked. I could hear Osak and the rest of the boys inside the barracks roaring with laughter. With as much gallantry as I could muster, I accepted the floral tribute and tried to strike up a conversation. Alas, Kvania was no conversationalist, but she seemed content to stare through the fence, big blue eyes as large as half dollars, in an almost maternal manner. Due to the lack of a reliable interpreter and the intervening barbed wire, which you must admit is quite a deterrent to true love, our affair petered out. For weeks she still smiled through the fence, but then some more eligible countryman must have displaced me in her affections, for I saw Kvania no more.

Toward the middle of June, Hank Conlin was taken quite ill and the *Inspektor* allowed me to take him to the *Lazarette* in Stolp. Conlin was one of the teamsters, a married man from Minetto, New York, and—with Olson, Chester Stough, and me—one of the four relative oldsters among our band of twenty. He was not a man to magnify matters and was in pretty rough shape by the time we turned him over to the Jerry medics at the *Lazarette*, where he was promptly hospitalized. The inevitable guard, Uncle Ben this time, went with us.

The *Lazarette* was a long, low building on the *Kaserne* grounds with one large waiting room and three cubicles at the far end, each staffed by a German army doctor. They tended to the lesser ailments and diagnosed prisoners, forced laborers, and German soldiers alike. The waiting room was fairly full when we arrived, but as Conlin was so obviously seriously ill, he was taken into the doctor's chamber ahead of the others. Ben and I waited outside with twenty other prisoners, two other guards, and seven French forced laborers. Most of these were in for bandaging and treatment of cuts, sprains, and the like. It was a well-known fact that there were quite a few malingerers among them and that the German doctors were openly corruptible. In talking with Schick on my previous visit, I found that many *Kommandos* had set up almost a roster as to whose turn it was to be sick. Once inside the doctor's room, a couple of packs of cigarettes could change hands and result in an official slip pronouncing the prisoner unfit to work for the next week. This was accepted practice, perfectly OK with Schick as long as it wasn't too badly overworked.

After a few minutes, Ben and I were called into the room and told that Conlin was going to be transferred to a large military hospital, also on the *Kaserne* grounds, and that he would be laid up for at least a month. The German doctor seemed quite a nice fellow and assured me that the hospital was competently staffed and that Conlin and any other prisoner patients got exactly the same treatment and attention as that extended to German army personnel. I also told the doctor about the boils we were plagued with at Benzin. He shook his head and said, "Unfortunately that is a condition widespread in this area." He gave me a fair-sized tube of ichthyol ointment and said it would help, though boils were inevitable in a country where everyone lived on potatoes to the virtual exclusion of any other food.

As I was leaving the *Lazarette*, I promised Conlin I would come in and see him whenever I could. Ben and I stopped off at Schick's to pick up a few items of clothing, and then set off for the Stolp railroad station. Arriving at the station, we found there would be quite an interval before the next train to Benzin. It was then that Ben asked, *"Johann, bist du Katholische or Evangelische?"* (Jack, are you Catholic or Protestant?) I told him I was a Protestant, which was also his faith, and he suggested we go to church to pass an hour. This was an incident I would long remember.

After you have been a soldier for a few weeks, your rifle becomes a part of you. It is like a mole or wart, something that you carry subconsciously. That's the way it was with Ben. We entered the church, a massive gray stone edifice two blocks from the station, and were halfway down the center aisle when the minister caught sight of us. Abandoning his text, he launched into a veritable tirade at poor old Ben, as devout a man as had ever set foot in the church. The gist of his remarks was that he was heartily ashamed of any German soldier with so little upbringing and decency that he would enter a house of God bearing arms. To make his point more pronounced, he commented that I, ostensibly an enemy, had sufficient sensibility not to make such a faux pas. This was hardly logical thinking, as it was unthinkable to picture a GI in the heart of Pomerania in 1944 strolling about in a house of God, or anywhere else for that matter, with a rifle slung over his shoulder. As it happened, there were only a handful of women in the congregation at this particular time. Nevertheless, Ben was overcome with embarrassment and confusion. We hustled back to the entry, stacked Ben's rifle (minus its firing pin) against the outer wall, and, thoroughly chastened, reentered. Poor old Ben was completely shaken. I had to console and reassure him all the way back to the station and on the train to Benzin that his actions were above reproach and that he was the unwitting victim of circumstances.

One morning, June 7, 1944, the guard came for us an hour later in the morning than usual. As soon as we were split up into working parties, we sensed that something was seriously wrong. The usually friendly German civilians were exceptionally quiet and at every opportunity would go off out of earshot and earnestly converse. We were all puzzled at their unusual behavior. A couple of the Frenchies caught our eye and gave us a grin and cautious wink, but it was not until the middle of the afternoon that we found out what had happened. Franz Mahn was working near me in a corner of the barn with no one else around at that moment. He quietly told me that a large-scale American and British landing had been made the previous day on the Normandy peninsula, that major German forces had engaged them, and that a tremendous battle was then in progress.

I passed the word on to the boys in the barracks that night, and they were sure a happy bunch. We all agreed that we would act exactly as before and in no way indicate to the Germans that we knew what had transpired. Of course, the Germans must have known that after the first day or so we knew, for they knew how close we were to the Frenchies, and the Frenchmen, with virtually as much freedom as the German civilians, were always posted on any new developments.

After three weeks in the hospital, Conlin rejoined us at the farm. Ben went in alone on the train to bring Hank back from

Stolp. Hank said the hospital care had been very good and that they had certainly done a good job of diagnosis and medication. While convalescing he had many opportunities to talk with other GIs, and they had confirmed that the war was going badly for the Germans on all fronts. In addition to the Allied Normandy landings, which they had been unable to contain, massive Russian onslaughts on a front more than a thousand miles long were chewing up German divisions in a relentless push to the west. In the barracks, the progress of the war was our prime topic of conversation. Once in a while we would get hold of the *Danziger Morgenpost* or the Swedish paper *Aftonbladet*, but we could glean little news from such sources. Our spoken German was pretty fair, but when it came to reading we were licked. They shied away from printing maps, and the place names mentioned were always those of hamlets so that no intelligible picture could be secured. No doubt when the *Wehrmacht* was roaring through Poland and the Low Countries, back in 1939 and 1940, the German press was not nearly so diffident and probably published large-scale maps every day indicating major European cities. These were different days now.

One Saturday night, the *Inspektor* came into the barracks and told me to have two of our boys take a wheelbarrow down to the *Gasthaus* the next morning to pick up a keg of beer. This was certainly an amazing turn of events. It was *Pfingsten* (Pentecost, a holiday celebrated much more widely in Germany than in the U.S.). The beer tasted first rate, and we had a pleasant Sunday.

CHAPTER 12

Barn Raising

As the summer wore on, the green fields of rye shoots literally sprang up, as did the vast acreages given over to turnips and potatoes. For several days, most of us were taken from our regularly assigned duties to work on the addition to the already mammoth barn facing our barracks. These barns were all-brick structures with slate roofs built to last for eternity. Some of the barns farther away from the farmyard had dates cut into the lintels, in Roman numerals, going back 300 years, and these barns looked every bit as sturdy as the more recent ones. The architecture was identical.

The German method of building barns was a real eye opener. Enormous 12-inch-by-12-inch carrying beams were laid out on the ground and carefully measured. At predetermined places, notches were cut with adzes to receive the cross members, 8-inch-by-8-inch rafters. Each piece in this giant structural assembly had chiseled a Roman numeral in it. It was, in effect, erector set technique, though strange in that there were no blueprints or master plans of any sort. Where beams or rafters joined, they were cut at the extremities to create tenon and mortise joints. For example, a 12-inch-by-12-inch beam would have 4 inches shaved off each side of the extreme end, leaving a 4-inch-thick middle projection. The beam in which it was to rest would be treated in reverse fashion, having a 4-inch-wide slot, or groove, chiseled in its center. Then the two members would be laid out on the ground in the precise relative positions they would assume when erected, and a hole would be drilled through the joint with a 2-inch wood bit. Two-inch diameter dowel pins of green hardwood were fashioned for later insertion. Absolutely no nails, screws, or metal fasteners of any sort were used.

The sidewall construction, commenced during my brief tenure tending mason, had long since been completed. The barn extension was some sixty feet in length and thirty-six to forty feet wide. One section had already been partitioned off by a masonry wall as a garage for the *Inspektor*'s postwar automobile. Nothing like looking ahead.

Using twenty-six men, the erection of the skeletal roof structure was completed in two days. First, the carrying beams across the narrower dimension were set into place in recesses built into the sidewalls. These were picked up by twelve men and held over their heads, while another dozen men with long, lancelike metal-tipped poles impaled the beam from below and raised it to the desired height of 18 feet. This was the touchy part of the job, with the great balk of timber wavering in the air supported entirely by six pairs of slender-tipped poles while it was slowly jockeyed into position.

Once the lowest row of crossbeams was positioned, we all went aloft to tie in the rafters and other supporting members. Pegged joints were malleted into place with the precut hardwood dowels as the roof began to take shape. Longitudinal members were set in the prepared notches. Everything went together perfectly, which was amazing, as during the ground layout work no protractors or precise measuring tools were used, just a common folding carpenter's rule. The barn had a gambrel roof, so it required a second set of horizontal beams. The hoisting of the second tier of beams was even more precarious than the first, for this time the pole holders were aloft themselves, and the timbers had to be gingerly transferred from one set of poles to another on several occasions. One slip and the massive timber would come crashing down, making mincemeat of any poor chap in its way. Needless to say we were all ultracareful, and no accidents took place.

The final, and most hazardous, step was lifting the giant ridgepole into place. The ridgepole was by far the heaviest piece of all, and it needed three pole transfers on its way up from the ground. Teetering in the air a good 45 feet above ground level, it was a sight to behold. With infinite patience, one end was worked into a hole that had been chiseled into the brick sidewall of the main barn. The other end was lowered between two notched rafters and the retaining pin driven through. The ridgepole was notched at regular intervals to receive additional angled rafters. Once the dowels were driven through these three-piece joints, the surplus pin stock was sawed off.

We finished up about 3:30 P.M., having erected a framework involving at least fifty major timbers with innumerable smaller tie braces and cross-struts. As soon as it was complete, the *Inspektor* ordered Hans up to the top of the ridgepole with a green wreath. This was some local good luck custom. In accordance with still another local tradition, we all knocked off work for the day, and the *Gasthaus* sent up a cask of beer. The next day we went back to our normal farm duties, while three Germans and one of the Frenchmen nailed light furring strips to the rafters and hung the curved red tiles forming the roof.

During most of this early period, I was a regular member of the woods crew, but frequently we would all be drafted for some special task for a few days. We were always glad to pick up our axes and get back in the woods again. Late in May we all spent a few days planting potatoes, and about June 20 there was another planting session, this time turnips. By July 1 we were extremely busy getting in the hay. About half the GIs were out in the fields loading the wagons, while the rest of us, with the exception of the teamsters, worked in the mammoth hay-storage barn. I was one of those on the dirty end of the stick, for I was in the barn crew, and the barn was a stifling place to work.

We used six wagons, which came in from the fields in a steady stream, loaded to overflowing with hay. We were on the second floor of the immense barn, standing directly beneath a big double door that resembled a skylight. The wagons were unloaded onto a leather endless belt device about ten feet wide, with rows of retaining spikes running across the width every ten feet to keep the hay from sliding back down the belt. The whole contraption stuck up in the air at a 45-degree angle and must have been all of ninety feet long. The terminus of the belt was directly above the wide-open hatchway doors.

We were standing in an enormous chamber some thirty feet below the opening, looking up at the sloping rafters as they ran together to meet the giant ridgepole. Four of us, two right-hand forkers and two left-hand forkers, formed a square about twelve feet away from each other, directly beneath the yawning hatchway. A line of four other forkers fanned out diagonally from the four original hay handlers to the extreme corners of the barn. These were mostly girls, some German, some Ukrainian. Once the belt started up, we had to fork like mad to the second in line, in a vain endeavor to keep the center area relatively clear.

It was a brutally hot day. The barn was practically airless, and we were being deluged by a constant Niagara of hay, thickly mingled with dust, pouring down on us from above. Within fifteen minutes from the first forkful we were all bathed in sweat. The heavy concentration of dust coated our bodies, filtered down our necks and backs, and reached deep into our throats, leaving us all gasping. No one in the barn was having a picnic, but the men beneath the hatchway took the worst beating. I had no aversion to the pitchfork, unlike the hoe, and was considered quite adept with this particular implement.

At 8:00 A.M. the wagons started rolling up in an endless procession. There was no letup, for before one wagon had been cleared, another stood in line waiting to be unloaded. We stopped only for an occasional gulp of water and a brief respite at 1:30 P.M. for a sandwich. The level of the hay underneath our feet rose steadily. By 7:30 P.M., we had filled the barn to overflowing. At the end, we were standing with our heads actually poking out of the loading doors. Tottering out of the barn, we looked like members of a blackface minstrel show.

No sooner was the haying done than we were put to work digging an enormous circular pit 40 feet in diameter and 20 feet deep. After two days of digging, our pit looked like the

Yale Bowl. If moon men had their telescopes focused on Ben-zin, they probably hailed the discovery of a new earth crater of the first magnitude.

As the pit was completed, wooden forms shaped in seg-ments of a circle were erected around the perimeter and joined to each other. The excavated dirt was partly used as backfilling behind the curved wooden forms. Then a central pole coming up to ground level was erected and a ramp set in place, down which a team of oxen was led to the bottom of the circular board-enclosed pit. The oxen were hitched to a hori-zontal pole secured by a ring to the vertical central pole. Soon wagon loads of heavy ensilage drew up to the pit, and it became clear that we had created an underground silo. The heavy crop, something like peas or beans, was forked into the silo, and the oxen tramping around in endless circles packed it down and compressed it with their hooves. After two days, much in the manner of our haying technique, the oxen had worked them-selves back up to natural ground level. Then we pulled out the central column with a primitive chain fall, spread a 2-foot layer of straw on top, and covered the entire circular area with a cou-ple of feet of dirt remaining from the original excavation pile. The whole thing had a strange unreal quality, like some Druid-built pagan pancake shrine. Our farm boys had never seen any-thing like this in their lives back in the States. I remember we had occasion to open up one of these underground storage bins later that winter, and a heavy fermented smell, like sour whiskey mash, rose to the heavens as the semidecomposed fod-der was exposed to the air.

Another time we spent a couple of days in a turnip field, which, in addition to the paying crop, had yielded an equal proportion of heavily nettled purple thistles. For this chore, we each had a hoe handle with a bladed tip like a wide wood chisel secured to the business end. The thistles were sheared off at ground level. Once in a while we would root up a turnip, peel it with a jack knife, and eat away at it like an ice cream cone. This was OK as long as one chewed each mouthful over and over. Eating one of these turnips in undue haste would make your stomach feel as though you had feasted on a collection of three-cornered stones.

About July 10, I made another trip into Stolp, once again with Hans and Uncle Ben. This time we loaded some coal for the return trip, and I stocked up with an eight-week supply of Red Cross parcels, some more clothes, a good batch of books, a dartboard, checkers, razor blades, a hair clipper, toothbrushes, and a king-sized frying pan. I had brought back only nineteen toothbrushes, which caused somewhat of a dilemma until Swede Olsen announced that he had the kind of teeth he could shine on the seat of his pants, and proved it by displaying his bridgework.

One time, a couple of the boys were feeling ripe for a little devilry, so they slipped through the barbed-wire fence late one night. This was no great trick, as the strands of wire were widely spaced and the guard always went directly to his room in the *Inspektor*'s house right after the 10:00 P.M. head count. Even so, it was relatively light out, despite the late hour, and I wasn't especially pleased about the escapade because it was for no important purpose and could easily have brought forth reprisals had they been detected. By this date, our door was no longer being locked at 10:00 P.M., so the boys slipped out the door and through the barbed wire to a barn where there stood two barrels of *Kartoffel Schnaps* (potato whiskey). For all its watery appearance, the *Schnaps* burned like molten lava as it went down. Somehow the boys had secured a small gimlet, which they used to drill a little hole in the side of one of the casks. The whiskey came out in a stream and filled up a couple of powdered milk cans. Once the cans were filled, they stopped the hole with a small wooden plug, just a little bigger around than the shaft of a wooden match. The plug was blackened to match the color of the barrel. Most of us were content with a sip or two, but the two rumrunners, elated about their exploit, tucked away several double shots, to their profound regret. A snootful of *Kartoffel Schnaps* hit like a sledgehammer the morning after. We never heard anything from the Jerries about this escapade, so they were either unaware of the shortage or blamed somebody else.

The haying completed, the woods crew got back to their normal duties, which we greatly preferred to the farming assignments. All of us took pride in being able to drop giant pines within six inches of a predetermined spot. Heinrich was a shrewd-enough psychologist to sense this and left us with a minimum amount of actual supervision. The woods crew was the upper strata of Benzin laborers, and we knocked off work about 6:00 P.M. even though many of the field gangs took full advantage of the lengthened days and toiled until 7:30 P.M. July gave way to August, but the long days were still with us.

The third week in August, there was another interval when we all left our regular duties and went on the rye harvest. Benzin devoted vast acreage to rye, the crop second in importance only to potatoes. The stalks were mechanically cut and bound, though much of the binder cord later broke. We were shown how to retie the bundle with a simple twist-over knot, using a few stalks in lieu of cord or twine. The second phase was the loading of the shocks on the wagons in the fields and the subsequent unloading at the designated barns. The relatively small oat and barley crops were also harvested during this period.

On August 21 came another trip to Stolp for food parcels and reading matter. This time I brought back an eight-week supply of Red Cross parcels, a few shirts, and some underwear. By good fortune, a shipment of books had arrived that very day from the *Stalag*, and I was able to have first pick. Three of the titles much enjoyed by the boys were *A Tree Grows in Brooklyn*, *H. M. Pulham, Esq.*, and *Sorrell and Son*.

On the return trip we ran into a light rain, and Uncle Ben took Hans and me into a roadside *Gasthaus* right across the main road from the airfield barracks. The base was a large fighter pilot training center, and many of those in the barroom were members of the *Luftwaffe*. I was greatly impressed by their extreme youth. Many of them were sixteen or seventeen.

The airfield paralleled the main road to the Benzin turnoff, and then bordered this lesser road for a couple of miles down to the railroad crossing. Most of the craft were rather old trainers, though there were a dozen new Messerschmitt Me 110 planes out on the runways that afternoon. I was very amused to see an ancient triplane circa World War I or thereabouts. The entire airfield was bordered by an anchor fence about twelve feet high.

Shortly before we arrived back in Benzin, a photographer took a group picture of the other nineteen American boys at the barracks. I believe this was done by the German army, though the purpose seems obscure. About a month later, we each received a print of this picture.

August 23 was a red-letter day for me. Old Ben came furiously pedaling his bike up the lane and ran up the path to the barracks, grinning from ear to ear, shouting "Johann, Johann, some letters from your *Mutter!*" I had received my first mail: two letters from my mother. The letters had traveled a circuitous route via Switzerland, *Stalag* VII A in Moosburg, Bavaria, *Stalag* II B in Hammerstein, Pomerania, and finally Benzin.

The most comforting thing about the letters was the knowledge that my earlier postcards from Italy and Moosburg had reached their destination. Now that communication had been established, it seemed reasonable to expect regular correspondence. The letters indicated that at least two food parcels and one cigarette parcel were en route. Two or three of the other boys also had their first contact with home in this batch of mail.

I was a happy fellow when I hit the hay (or to be technically correct, straw) that night. Indeed, we were all feeling pretty good. An ample stock of parcel food was on hand, we had a good guard, we were on the best of terms with Ukes, Frenchmen, Poles, and Germans alike, and our work had become so second nature we took it in stride. To cap it all, the war news was better and better all the time, and now we had forged a link with our loved ones back home.

By this time, we were all so fluent in *Platt Deutsch* (Low German) that we had no difficulty in conversing on most normal topics. Our words were correct and our pronunciation beyond reproach, but we persisted in literally substituting the German equivalent for a given English word, so our sentence structure was highly amusing to the Germans. They were all loud in their praise of our flawless pronunciation, and everyone seemed to take a lot of pride in the fact that we were, in a sense, their protégés. They all agreed that we were far more fluent in four months than the Frenchies who had been there four years. I suppose a great deal of this was because we were all quite young and keenly interested in learning how to speak a foreign tongue. Then, too, I'm convinced that it is far simpler task for an English-speaking person to pick up German than anyone whose mother tongue is a Romance language. There is a very great affinity in pronunciation, particularly such words as *Axe* (axe), *Butter* (butter), *guten Morgen* (good morning), *gute Nacht* (good night), and *Mutter* (mother).

Our friends, the Frenchmen, made a practice of coming over to our barracks for an hour most Sunday afternoons. They were always very appreciative of the occasional gifts of food we gave them. Without exception, we found them polite, considerate, and sincere. Many times we almost had to insist that they take the prunes, cigarettes, or whatever it was we wanted them to have. From them we learned some of the intricacies of chess, and they were quite taken with the American game of horseshoes, which neither they nor the Germans had ever seen anyone play before.

CHAPTER 13

High Interest in American Politics

Americans, or ground troops at any rate, were fairly well thought of in Benzin. There was a steady tirade on the German radio about the inhumanity of British and American airmen and their indiscriminate bombings of helpless women and children in German cities. Of course, this story couldn't stand much scrutiny if one recalled Coventry, Rotterdam, Plymouth, and the other cities blitzed by Göring, but it was convenient to forget that the shoe used to be on the other foot. And so the airwaves spewed forth the continuing tales of barbarous bombing raids.

With the exception of the air force, Americans were regarded as essentially good people who had been led down the wrong path by a lack of understanding of the true causes of the war. This supposed misconception was assisted to no end by the Jewish-dominated U.S. press, and aided and abetted by the connivance of Winston Churchill and the *Jude* (Jew) Roosevelt. They insisted on pronouncing his name "Rosenfeld," and no amount of talk could convince them that he was a *Nederlander* (Dutch), and about a sixth generation one at that.

Eisenhower was a real puzzler to them. They knew that the name was certainly of German origin and couldn't quite understand how he got on the "wrong team." This German belief that Americans were well-meaning, misinformed, misguided souls also embraced the Canadians, and in only a slightly lesser degree the rank and file British.

The Russians and the Poles were the real villains in the piece. The Germans' hatred toward these races was virulent, matched only by their loathing of the Jews. The Jews were despised by all true Party members, and Benzin had its full share, who had committed to memory all of the Party literature and catchphrases telling how the Jews had economically strangled the Third Reich prior to the timely arrival of the Führer and his drastic policies. Russians and Poles were seriously titled "subhumans." Allied prisoners were treated with kid gloves compared to the barbaric treatment meted out to the Russians, who even in their final hours were denied basic medical attention.

In trying to rationalize this widespread belief that the Americans were basically pretty good people, I concluded that one definite factor was the waves of German migration to the States, both before and after World War I, and the subsequent letters to those left behind in the Fatherland. In addition, the U.S. had been magnanimous in the aftermath of World War I, seeking no territorial spoils and advocating an extremely mild reparations policy, followed by large-scale economic assistance. As a result, though we were on opposite sides of the fence, the U.S. had fairly good press in Germany in 1944.

Indeed, this opinion in the last few weeks of the war, when the inevitable outcome was apparent even to the Nazi fanatics, crystallized into a firm fixation that the Allies and the Germans would conclude an honorable truce in the West, then join hands in a mighty crusade to the East to stamp out Bolshevism from the face of the earth. This dream of joining forces was accepted almost as an inescapable fact in those last bleak weeks. It could be termed wishful thinking, yet it was apparently something that sprang from the people, as to my knowledge it was not a belief planted, or even fostered, by the Bureau of Propaganda.

The Germans have always been typified as first and foremost a logical people, though at Benzin there was an incident where their logic was too elementary and led to totally incorrect conclusions. I was amused, in August 1944, to have so many German civilians pose numerous questions about Wendell

Willkie and his chances of winning the U.S. presidential election. After asking a few questions of my own, the motivation behind their sudden interest in American politics became transparently clear. They had reduced the election to logic in its simplest terms. Rosenfeld, *"der Jude,"* was a warmonger and necessarily represented the U.S. "War Party." Willkie was his opponent, and necessarily must be diametrically opposed to everything that Rosenfeld advocated. This basic premise clearly established, it followed that Willkie must head up the "Peace Party" and, by inference, at least, be a friend of Germany. No doubt this made a lot of sense to the Germans, but it was hilarious to the Benzin GIs. We knew we could never convince the Jerries of the true state of affairs, so we implied that their conclusions were not far off the mark. They were quite crestfallen when Rosenfeld later won the election, but salvaged some solace in the fact that Willkie had polled so many millions of votes, which to them still held out hopes for the ultimate downfall of Rosenfeld. How little they knew of the American political scene and the unshakeable resolve of both parties to pursue the war with unrelenting vigor.

All through August we had heard of fabulous Russian advances along the entire Eastern Front, and a great deal about the Polish uprising in Warsaw led by General Bor-Komorowski. The Russians were well across the Vistula, and the Warsaw insurrection seemed to indicate a further collapse of the German defense perimeter. By now we knew of the Allied landing in the South of France and that the Normandy forces had driven beyond Paris.

I am sure that most of our boys never gave any thought to the actual mechanics by which their own personal liberation would be accomplished. They knew that the war was going favorably for the Allies but didn't make a personal equation of it. Hank Conlin and I, being a few years older than the rest, held certain convictions and apprehensions in this regard, which we didn't voice to the others. It was our firm belief that if the German authority held its grip until a peace treaty had been signed, and if we were still in the protective custody of the

Wehrmacht, that we would come out all right. On the other hand, if civil authority collapsed in the final weeks, we could easily be swept up in a bloodbath triggered by a panic-stricken wave of mob violence.

It wasn't the Benzin villagers that we feared, but an embittered, undisciplined retreating army. Such a mob, hands already steeped in blood and answerable to no one, would think little of knocking off a few more enemies of the Reich. This would be particularly true if these roving bands were SS men. We felt so strongly about this possibility that we resolved to try to get our hands on civilian clothing if such a situation ever began to materialize.

Another big factor in our thinking was the likelihood that we would be liberated from the east. Knowing well that Russian infantrymen were trained to shoot first and ask questions later, we might have to lie low, at least until after the first waves of troops has passed beyond Benzin.

In the end, neither of these scenarios came to pass, but I still think it was prudent to do some basic planning along these lines.

CHAPTER 14

Potatoes, Potatoes

September came in with a week of unseasonably cool weather. Mail now came, for some, at least once a week, and the only distasteful chore looming up was the potato harvest. The Frenchies assured us we were in for five weeks of back-breaking labor.

The potato harvest lived up to advance notice. Beginning on September 24, it was the hardest five weeks of concentrated unending labor that I have ever put in, before or since. There were at least four hundred acres given over solely to potatoes at Benzin, with about half this acreage devoted to red potatoes. The yield, in bushels per acre, startled our farm boys, who contended it doubled any figures attained in the U.S.

Everyone in Benzin, with the exception of the smith and Franz Mahn, was put on the potato harvest. The rotary digger would go down the rows loosening the soil and exposing the spuds for the pickers. Then a long line of forty individuals, each working a dual row, would walk along picking up potatoes from both sides and tossing the spuds into a large basket set on the ground immediately ahead. The technique was to set the basket up ahead about fifteen feet, working toward it and tossing the picked spuds from a crouched position. When you reached the basket, you moved it ahead again and repeated the process. Three or four people were assigned to remove the full baskets and replace them with empties so the picking process could go on uninterrupted. The only chance to straighten up came at those intervals when you had to cart the basket up ahead.

Bending over to ground level, or even below, for hours at a stretch was a real backbreaker. The old army cry "Oh, my aching back" never rang more true. Returning to the barracks in the evenings in a semiape position, we seriously feared we might grow that way permanently. Anyone with a Sloan's Liniment concession in Benzin during those five weeks would have made a fortune.

After three days, I abandoned the approved method and went in for progressing exclusively on my knees. The ground was damn cold, especially when it had rained during the night, and some days I moved literally miles in the mud, on my knees all the while. Mornings, before leaving the barracks, I would wrap my knees in strips of an old blanket. Even so, my knees were badly swollen most of the time, and the Germans all urged me to give it up, pointing out that I was courting the hazards of arthritis and rheumatism.

The formation was an odd one. A long line of pickers started from an edge of the field. First were about twenty German girls, then the six Uke maidens, followed by the Frenchies, with the GIs on the end of the line. As we progressed down the 500-foot rows, the line would assume a 45-degree angle. The German girls, picking as though they were gleaning gold nuggets, would reach the end of their rows by the time the Ukes had hit the 75 percent mark, the Frenchies the midpoint, and the hopelessly outclassed GIs the 30 percent mark. This brought forth roaring and cursing from the *Inspektor* and much amusement on the part of Hans and the Germans driving the wagons or emptying the filled baskets. The German girls would then start working to meet us from the opposite end of our assigned rows and we would be hard-pressed to meet them at midfield. Similarly, the Uke girls would bail out the Frenchies by doing about a quarter of their assigned rows. The pattern was always the same.

The Germans had an incentive bonus plan, giving a ticket for each basket picked. The girls just knocked themselves out trying to earn as many tickets as they possibly could, and for that reason were not loath to do large stretches of the rows nominally assigned to our GIs. I was reamed out three or four times by the *Inspektor* before he realized we were giving it all we had, but just didn't have any talent at all for picking potatoes.

Those were our most miserable days at Benzin. Oh, how we hated potatoes. First we had eaten them at least twice a day for the past five months, resulting in a plague of boils. Now we were making pretzels of our spines picking up the goddamned things. As we would finally wind up a field with a sigh and sense of accomplishment, we would be led off to some other tract the size of an airport to begin all over again.

I stayed on the assignment for four of the five weeks involved. Finally, in despair—for while the GIs collectively were the worst pickers, I was individually the worst of them—the *Inspektor* transferred me to the task of storing the spuds. There was a mesh wire sifter in the field, and all the potatoes were brought to this machine in the baskets from the pickers and dumped in the hopper. Two screens moving in opposite directions sorted out the large ones from the small, shaking off most of the dirt in the process. The spuds then poured out, segregated, from two hoppers in steady streams. The larger ones, destined for the *Wehrmacht,* were loaded into wagons and driven down to the Benzin rail siding, where we loaded them into boxcars with potato forks. The smaller ones were loaded in other wagons and driven off to an adjacent field. This was no picnic, but it beat the hell out of picking.

After the army spuds had all been loaded, I became a member of the potato storage crew. The medium-sized potatoes were buried in long trenches for storage, in similar fashion to the underground silo plan used for ensilage. The first step was to dig a trench about thirty inches deep and twelve feet wide. This trench was generally about four hundred feet long and was lined with plank forms on both sides. The dirt was heaped up on one side, and then a layer of straw was spread in the bottom of the trench. The laden wagons were driven up a ramp alongside the trench. The ramp was pitched sharply toward the trench so that when the wagon sideboard was removed, the entire load spilled into the trench. Bit by bit, the pile of spuds formed a long pyramid about ten feet high at the apex. Then on went two feet of straw. The originally removed dirt was heaped on top and packed with the backs of the shovels. The end result was a long dirt pyramid something like you'd see in pictures of ancient breastworks in medieval wars. This also was an eye opener to our farm boys, who were totally unfamiliar with such a method of potato storage.

On October 17, during the latter part of the potato harvest, I went into Stolp with Uncle Ben for more food parcels. This was my last trip of this nature with Ben, who would be replaced on November 15 by a new guard. We went by train in the early afternoon. Hans had left early in the morning with the wagon, and we were to join him only for the purpose of loading up for the return trip; then Ben and I were to come back by train.

I said it was my last trip to Stolp with Ben, and it was, but if there had been any German army officers in the Benzin railroad station that afternoon, it would surely have been Ben's last trip anywhere. We had gone into the country station on one of our wagons, bringing potatoes to the rail siding for loading. Just as we arrived at the waiting room, Ben remembered some papers he had forgotten back in his room. These were for his superior at Stolp and probably had something to do with his impending transfer. Ben was very upset, for he would get quite a reaming if he didn't show up at headquarters on time, and now he would get the same reception if he showed up without the documents. Fortunately, we had about an hour to wait for the train, so Ben decided to borrow a bicycle and make a flying trip back to the farm for the missing papers. It was going to be an awful close thing, but Ben had no other option if he was to escape from the situation without a real blistering.

As soon as Ben borrowed the bike, he took off hell for leather. Without thinking, he'd handed me his rifle. There I was in the waiting room of the Benzin railroad station, rigged out in an 1870 French uniform, holding Ben's rifle. Not wanting to start a panic or get Ben in trouble, I leaned the damn thing up against the wall and sat on a bench as far away as possible. Fortunately there were only a few housewives waiting for the train, and Ben's faux pas went unnoticed. About five minutes before the train was due to pull out, old Ben skidded into the station yard and came puffing up to me, his face wreathed in smiles. I didn't mention his mental lapse in entrusting his weapon to the enemy, and it never occurred to him that his behavior had been a wee bit irregular. Poor old Ben just wasn't cut out to be a military man.

The visit with Jack Schick was most encouraging. We loaded the wagon with an eight-week supply of parcels, including the long-heralded Christmas parcels, which were reputed to contain a plum pudding, a jar of honey, and other delicacies. The war news was equally stimulating. The Italian front was a virtual stalemate, but everywhere else tremendous advances were being made. France and Belgium were practically cleared of Germans. In the east, Romania and Bulgaria had been liberated, and another massive Russian offensive threatened to kick off at any time in the Polish sector of the line. Each trip to Stolp, with assurances of food supplies, clothing, and above all reliable war news, was like a tonic to all of us at Benzin.

At long last, by November 1 we were all done harvesting the potatoes. What a pleasure it was to get back to our normal duties again.

The mail continued to come in at a good rate. Most of us could now expect at least one letter a week, which was a great lift to morale. Unfortunately, there were two or three boys in the barracks who never did receive any mail, but even they always lived in hopes that the next time Ben came up the path there would be something for them.

November 8 was a tremendously exciting day in the barracks: John Benson and Jess McDonald received food parcels from home. They were almost moved to tears, but with the generous, selfless attitude that had typified our entire stay at Benzin, they wanted to share some of their good fortune with the rest of us. Needless to say, we all refused their offers, but it was the spirit that counted. On November 12, I broke through with a package of three cartons of Camels.

Old Ben was as delighted to bring the packages as we were to receive them. How many times since have I marveled at his implicit honesty, for there were no receipts, no signing of any kind, and Ben, had he chosen, could have intercepted all of these parcels, and we would have been none the wiser. Remember, this was Germany in 1944, where coffee, cigarettes, jam, and chocolate bars, to civilian and *Wehrmacht* alike, were seen only in hazy, golden memories of happier days gone by. We would never have known of any interceptions, and even if we had, there certainly was no one to whom we could have effectually protested. It would surely have been a strong temptation to almost anyone but Ben.

A week after the potato harvest was completed, *Herr Inspektor* came into the barracks on Sunday afternoon and made a big ceremony of paying us. We all gave him our potato picking tickets (one per basket), which he totaled. I was low man on the totem pole with 1,138. A couple of the boys had as many as 1,675. Apparently the Geneva Convention had prescribed some nominal payment for work performed, which, in the case of captured Germans in the U.S., had some merit, as they could buy combs, cigarettes, wallets, and other articles with the money. In Germany, special scrip called *Gefangene Gelt* (prison money) was used to cover the regulation, but the gesture was meaningless, as the stuff was not accepted by merchants. For all practical purposes, we might as well not have been paid at all. Nevertheless, the *Inspektor* insisted on going through this farcical procedure, and even supplemented our regular salary with bonus money based on the amounts we had picked. With much pomp our names were called out, we stepped up to receive the loot, and our names were duly checked off in the tally book.

Later in the day, the money showed up in the poker game, and Hank Conlin, after several hot hands, was the possessor of some 222,000 marks in *Gefangene Gelt*. The whole affair was ridiculous and the humor of it was not lost on our boys.

Johnny DiCrecchio amused us one day by stating that although the Germans ate, drank, lived, and breathed potatoes, he had found out by inquiry that in Pomerania, at least, potato chips were unknown. He contended that in about ten years, which was how long he calculated it would take for him to overcome his revulsion to potatoes, he would come back to Benzin with a couple of barrels of salt and some cellophane bags and set up a potato chip factory. It was an interesting speculation at any rate.

Once we were back at our regular tasks, there was again a social atmosphere in the barracks during the evenings. Without exception, during the spud harvest, we had all toppled into bed a half hour after chow. Now the books came down off the shelf once more, the card games resumed, and conversation flourished. We had a couple of comedians among the lot and a full measure of hillbilly ballads accompanied on the spoons. Arch Blevins and Delbert Kinder had a fondness for "Wabash Cannonball," "Little Darlin' of the Ozarks," "No Letter Today, Dear," and various other plaintive crimes in the name of music. Jim Pierce, William Halvorsen, and Daniel Henderson were a good trio on some of the old standby hymns. Particularly on Sundays, these boys would team up on "Rock of Ages," "Abide With Me," "Lead Kindly Light," and other standards and did a real good job of it. Vocalists were generally accompanied by comb-and-tissue-paper artists and, if the tempo was right, by some brisk spoon work.

CHAPTER 15

48 Kilos (106 Pounds)

By mid-October it had begun to darken earlier in the evenings, and by November 10 it was quite dark by 5:00 P.M. Accordingly, our work day was shortened to 4:00, and on December 10 we stopped work by 3:30.

On November 14, we were taken to a neighboring small town to receive typhus inoculations. This was a merry trip, especially for the rest of the boys, for it was their first excursion out of Benzin since their arrival. The town where the shots were to be given was eight miles away, in the opposite direction from Stolp, so it was new country to me also. Hans drove one wagon and Henderson the other. Both Hans and Ben had a good trip, for we kept them well supplied with cigarettes during the ride. The actual shots were given in a community hall, which I later found out was the local Nazi Party headquarters, by a team of three medics sent out from the *Stalag*. This town had been selected as one of the focal points because it was the hub of about eight *Kommandos*. There was no great hurry, for the day was shot anyway and neither Ben nor Hans was in any great sweat to get back to Benzin. The shots took a matter of minutes, and then we all had a chance to exchange gossip with the eighty-odd prisoners who had converged on the hall. It was a pleasant departure from routine.

The medics had a scale with them, and I was shocked when I weighed in at 48 kilos (106 pounds). I knew I had lost a great deal of weight, but never realized it had gone to this extent. The rest of the boys were also running fifty or more pounds below their normal prewar weights. In all truth, however, despite the fact we must have looked like animated beanpoles, all of us were in good health. We certainly couldn't have been accused of being flabby, and I know that my capabilities for manual labor, particularly lifting, were never better.

Uncle Ben left Benzin on November 15 and came in to shake hands all around before he left. We all hoped he was not being posted to active duty. Most likely he was merely being rotated to another *Kommando* assignment, for we had learned that it was standard practice to rotate guards at least once every four months.

The new guard checked in at the *Inspektor's* house on November 15, but we did not meet him until the following morning. He was a small man in his late fifties, a rather gnome-like figure with a long thin nose, watery blue eyes, and a limp. After a day or two, we had "Shorty" pretty well sized up. Like his predecessors, he was no eager beaver, just a German sad sack sweating out the rest of the war and thankful that he was able to do it in the tranquility of Benzin, a million miles removed from the harsh realities of combat and privation. As long as we caused him no grief, we could expect to continue our old routine with a bare minimum of supervision. As we came to know him better, we learned that though he had little to say, he had quite a sense of humor and enjoyed any sallies on the part of the boys.

One day, I was alone in the barracks piling up some Red Cross parcels when he came in. The boxes had "V2" stamped on the carton as a size or model designation. This was during the period when the new German V2 flying bombs were raising such havoc in London and Antwerp. Looking about to be sure he wasn't overheard, Shorty pointed to the stamp and softly said, "I think the American V2 is better than the German V2." His eyes twinkled as he spoke. Like our two previous guards, he had a fondness for American cigarettes. In such situations, as any ex-prisoner can attest, the cigarette can be a more powerful weapon than the rifle. He was a quiet little fellow, but we never felt the same friendship for him that we had for Ben.

With the end of the potato harvest, the work pace slacked off, and though we still turned out a good day's work by any standards, the furious drive of the harvesting period was a thing of the past. The quotas had generally been met, and even the *Inspektor* mellowed a bit as the field workers turned to fairly minor maintenance tasks such as splitting kindling and mending harnesses.

Toward the end of November, one day was set aside as surplus distribution day. All of the teamsters were employed in delivering the prescribed quantities of rye, potatoes, and lesser crops to each of Benzin's houses. Most of the rest of us were detailed to load the wagons from the main farm barns, then ride with the load to the workers' homes and unload the amounts of food that had been assigned under the share basis. This was a pleasant task, for we were sincerely glad that there had been surpluses to distribute. In several of the homes we were given a glass of beer, and Gustave Topel handed me a few slices of *Speck*, a kind of bacon, after we piled up his potatoes in his loft.

It was now bitterly cold at dawn when our woods crew, bundled up in overcoats and scarves, strode through Benzin on our way to the woods. Once we began swinging the axes, though, we found we could peel right down to our shirts and even unbutton our shirt collars without any discomfort. You had to keep chopping, though, for the moment you stopped, you practically froze in your tracks.

About 11:30 A.M., Heinrich would delegate one of us to get a fire going. Starting with dry pine twigs, we would have a roaring blaze by noontime, when we all knocked off for a sandwich. Sometimes we would bring a jar of Nescafé with us, melt snow in a saucepan, and wash our lunch down with some steaming coffee. Heinrich, a great coffee lover, as were all other Benzinians, was in favor of this idea.

In early December, we were cutting pitprops [wooden beams used to support the roof of a mine], all of which had to be exactly 2 meters long. Johnny DiCrecchio indulged in some minor sabotage one day, when Heinrich was out of the way, by sawing about two inches off the official measuring pole. He smudged up the sawed end with dirt, and for the rest of the day we dutifully sawed up dozens of undersized pitprops.

Late in the afternoon, old Heinrich tumbled that something was wrong and measured the stick against some props we had cut the preceding day. His face, normally red, grew livid, his eyes bulged, and we thought he was going to explode on the spot. We were all busily engaged, eyes averted, trying to appear nonchalant and entirely unaware that anything was amiss. After staring at us, in turn, for a couple of minutes, old Heinrich apparently decided he would never be able to determine just which one of us was the guilty party, so he said nothing. Of course, he could have reported the matter to the *Inspektor*, who doubtless would have made it rough for the whole twenty of us, but by doing so Heinrich would surely come in for a real reaming himself. Next morning we had a new 2-meter stick, which Heinrich checked about once an hour with a folding carpenter's rule he had brought along in his pocket. The incident was never mentioned by any of the parties concerned, and we never did know how Heinrich explained away the matter of the too-short props. He probably went out into the woods himself the following Sunday, chopped them into shorter pieces, and stacked them in one of the cordwood piles.

One day, we dropped three tremendous trees that had to be carted to the sawmill and sawed into planks or beams. The next morning we carried a curious contraption and some lengths of chain out to the site. The apparatus was a boxlike wooden framework about twelve feet high with two rows of staggered drilled holes on the two vertical members. In addition, we had a long handle, like a well sweep, and two pairs of steel spikes joined together with a few links of chain.

It turned out the contraption was a primitive jack, and it functioned amazingly well. The first step was to scoop out the dirt under one end of the giant log and snake a length of chain around the butt about three feet in from the end. This done, the boxlike affair was firmly set in the ground adjacent to the chain now encircling the log and braced with three small trees set up in tripod fashion. Next, the long handle piece was inserted through the two open ends of the pierced jack structure and the ends of the log chain fastened through a forged steel loop on the end of the handle. A steel pin was then pushed through the bottom pair of holes and the companion pin in the next higher hole in the second of the two rows of holes. Three boys on the end of the handle put their full force on the lever thus created. When the log came up an inch or so, all of the weight was on the higher of the two pins. This was the moment to draw out the lower pin and move it up one hole, where the process was repeated. Soon one end of the log was up in the air about forty inches, and two metal-bound wagon wheels mounted on an axle were rolled underneath. We slacked off the jack by reversing the pin sequence. When the log was resting on the axle, we went to the other end of the log and repeated the process. The logs formed the bed of the wagon and were arranged in a pyramid, two on the bottom and one on top wedged in between the bottom two.

The whole operation went smoothly, and we were all loaded in two hours. The logs were 50-footers, so we didn't have much of a turning radius, and Hans had to drive carefully to negotiate the winding road to the sawmill. I was chosen to go with Hans while Heinrich and the rest of the woods crew moved on to a new cutting area. Hans drove the team astride the top log and I straddled the log a couple of feet farther back. As the team walked along, Hans told me he had received his papers to report to Stolp for army duty on November 25.

The sawmill was about five miles from Benzin along a narrow secondary road. We neither met nor passed any other wagons or vehicles during the entire trip. This was not especially unusual. On our wagon trips to Stolp—along what was considered a fairly important road—we seldom met more than one or two fellow travelers until we joined the major highway at the airport junction for the last four miles into town. Even on this main artery, there was no traffic problem, and cyclists and wagons outnumbered the few motor trucks. I suppose this was primarily due to the absolute impossibility of procuring gasoline or diesel fuel for any but the most vital cargos. In Stolp itself, a fair-sized city, practically the only cars around were military vehicles.

On the way to the sawmill, the road passed the estate of the baron who, in the prewar era, had owned the vast Benzin acreage and been its unquestioned authority. His manor was an impressive turreted and gabled house set well back from the road and surrounded by large gardens now overgrown and sadly in need of attention. A curving drive led up to the house, going past a pond complete with half a dozen swans. The entire picture was of faded grandeur, a page from an era in German history destined for inevitable extinction.

Soon the sawmill came into view, a long shedlike building huddled at the side of a fast-flowing stream. The stream was dammed right by the mill and broadened into a millpond below the overshot wooden waterwheel. The ground rose in a gentle slope from the mill and stream, and it was to this slope that Hans drove the wagon. We halted about two hundred fifty feet from the mill, and Hans unhitched the team of horses and led them into a grove of trees. I was left alone for ten minutes while Hans went down to the mill, returning with two men each carrying metal-tipped barbed poles. The unloading method was simplicity itself. Two two-man teams inserted 4-inch diameter poles through the wheel spokes, lifting upward against the axle hubs. At a given signal, both teams heaved and the logs, wheels and all, toppled over. Bear in mind that we were on an inclined hillside, exerting pressure solely from the high side and getting a lot of help from gravity. As the logs passed the point of no return, for one split second the entire tremendous weight was borne entirely by two metal-bound wooden wagon wheels. I was sure they would crumple under the fearful strain.

In a second it was all over. The logs were on the ground, and the wheels, spinning crazily, were chained atop the logs. Their relative positions had changed in the twinkling of an eye. In a trice the chains were loosed and the two axle assemblies rolled off into the grove where the team was grazing. Then, two men to each end, we rolled the first log down to the low-roofed mill. Once started, the log rolled easily, and we used the cant hooks, or peavies, primarily to brake and to see that one end didn't get ahead of the other. As the log neared the building, an entire hinged wall section was raised from within. In this manner the log rolled, pretty much by its own momentum, right onto the saw table. The other two logs followed in short order, and by 3:00 P.M. we were on our way back to Benzin, making fair time for the trip as the team only had to pull the two closely coupled axle assemblies.

CHAPTER 16

Christmas

On December 9, I received my first food package from home. Everything in life is relative. A crude bed of straw to a man who has slept in mud for weeks, the sight of a fellow man to one alone in the Arctic—these are the reactions of a prisoner to such wonderful delicacies as Jell-O pudding powders, a box of biscuit mix, a can of Crisco, and a pound of tea. Another item, which would serve me in good stead on our later trek, was two pairs of heavy woolen socks. No value, however fantastic, could be placed on such treasures. Then there was the sentimental aspect. These items, packed with loving care, had been sent by my mother. Her dear hands had tied these strings. I know that every prisoner fortunate enough to have received a package from home must have felt an emotional wallop down to his toes.

Ten days later, our woods crew brought back to the barracks our Christmas tree, a well-formed young spruce earmarked for this special purpose since early November. The tree was decorated that night with cigarette tinfoil and twisted metal strips saved from the key-opened Klim and corned beef cans from our Red Cross parcels. At a meeting in the barracks that night, we voted to issue the cherished Christmas parcel in addition to the regular issue. This was a calculated risk, but Schick had assured me that all of the other *Kommandos* in the area were adopting this practice because the parcel stocks at Stolp were ample. After all, Christmas came but once a year, and the war news had been so very encouraging of late. We were all convinced that the end must come soon. As I recall, the vote was unanimous on the double issue.

On the morning of December 18, the Germans were acting in a very odd manner, reminiscent of their behavior in the wake of the D-Day news, but this time there was an air of pronounced elation in their low-voiced conclaves. Once again, it was Franz Mahn who enlightened us. German field marshal Gerd von Rundstedt had launched a savage assault on the American lines in the Luxembourg sector and was rapidly slicing through into the rear echelon areas. A major breakthrough was imminent, with chaos in store for the Allied invaders. This was certainly disconcerting news.

Undaunted, we went ahead with our Christmas plans, and as the days progressed, we heard from the Frenchies that the German push, though serious, had lost much of its initial impetus and the front was being stabilized. On Christmas Eve, several of the Frenchmen came over, and we amazed Shorty and a few civilians within earshot by giving a fair to middling rendition of "Stille Nacht," in German no less. The *Inspektor*'s wife heard us from her living room, and soon after we were all asked to go down to the main house to sing a few carols. The rest were all in English, for we had shot our bolt on "Stille Nacht," though when we sang "Maryland, My Maryland," for good measure we swapped "Tannenbaums" for "Marylands."

We stayed at the *Inspektor*'s house about fifteen minutes and were each treated to a glass of wine. We always had a good opinion of the *Inspektor*'s wife, as she gave our cook a few peas, carrots, or beans whenever the opportunity presented itself— that is to say, anytime she was sure the *Inspektor* was a long way off the premises. She was as patently afraid of the *Inspektor* and his tantrums as any of the field hands. None of us envied her lot in life.

Christmas Eve 1944 was a night that none of the Benzin GIs will ever forget. We issued the supplementary special parcel about seven o'clock and were delighted with the contents: a jar of honey, a can of turkey meat, a bottle of maraschino cherries, nuts, plum pudding, dates, sausage, real butter, a flannel face cloth, and a pipe. The parcel was the same dimensions as our regular issue, so these naturally had to be small containers, but with all this and our regular parcel issue to boot, we were in for a week of feasting. By eight o'clock we were all singing and laughing, for this was indeed our happiest night in captivity. It was just as well that we extracted the fullest pleasure, for there were grim days to come.

The question of escape, usually paramount in prison tales, never really received any serious consideration from our group. The reasons for this, I think, were varied and sound. First, we knew that in Pomerania, practically on the Baltic coast, we were hundreds of miles from the only possible haven, Switzerland. Then too, although our German was intelligible, we had no illusions that we could ever convince anyone that we were natives. Other vital factors were a complete lack of money, no civilian clothing, and most important of all, no identity cards and papers. In Germany during these times, men in our age group not in uniform were rare indeed and would surely raise questions. Identity cards were an absolute essential for any traveler, whether he used rail facilities or was on foot. Cards were checked on every train, at every depot, and at established checkpoints along all major highways. With no money, the limited amount of food that we would start out with would soon be depleted, with no possible means of replenishment. Any trip to Switzerland, entirely on foot with neither map nor compass, would require at least sixty days, especially if we moved only by night. This posed another seeming impossibility: Where could we hope to hole up in the daytime?

The British were perpetually making escape efforts, but in virtually all cases they were supported by well-organized escape committees who provided clothing, money, and forged documents. Even so, those who actually made it to freedom were a pitifully small fraction, less than one in a thousand.

We concluded that if native-born German Jews, with all their inherent advantages regarding money and documentation, and no linguistic difficulties, were unable to quit the country (and the bulging concentration camps attested to their inability), what chance did a GI have?

Another equally important factor was the favorable turn that the war had taken since our capture. Had this been 1940, after the Dunkirk debacle, or 1942, with Rommel at the gates of Alexandria, no doubt our thinking would have been different. As it was, it seemed foolhardy to take such a monumental risk when events pointed to impending Allied victory. All we had to do was sweat it out for another few weeks—months at the most—for certain deliverance.

The German jubilation at the turns of events in the west diminished, and by January 9 we knew that the table had been turned and the Jerries were on the receiving end again. On January 10, I made my first trip into Stolp with Shorty, and this time Helmut drove the wagon, as Hans by now was a private in the *Wehrmacht.* Indeed, casualties being what they were, he could perhaps have already made sergeant. It was a known fact that training was a thing of the past in the German army in those days. Raw recruits were being thrown into the lines wherever the need was greatest. It was possible to be a civilian one day and three weeks later be deep in Poland manning a machine gun.

Schick's news was heartening. The Russians were really on the move and had sliced well into East Prussia. It was rumored that entrenchments were being hastily dug no more than fifty miles to the east of Stolp by Ukrainian and Polish slave laborers. Blackout regulations were being stringently enforced in Stolp, and ack-ack emplacements were being set up around the city's perimeter.

With things coming to a crescendo on all fronts, Schick was adopting a policy of larger parcel issues. We loaded a nine-week supply on our wagon, as well as three pairs of shoes, two overcoats, six shirts, and twenty pairs of socks.

On our way back to Benzin, we passed quite close to the railway station, and I could see it was ringed with ack-ack guns. Each battery was surrounded by a wall of sandbags. A half-dozen dreaded SS men were herding a crowd of scarecrows dressed in pajama-like purple-and-white striped outfits over to newly selected positions. This was my first look at concentration camp inmates, and as we were some distance away, my only impression was one of extreme emaciation. Later I was to have a firsthand meeting with these poor dregs of humanity and their arrant, callous, jackbooted SS captors.

When we went out to the woods a few days later, we found that our six-man GI crew and overseer Heinrich had been supplemented by four German soldiers. They had all seen recent service on the Russian front, and to this day I don't know the reasons for their stay in Benzin. It may have been that the woods work was felt to be some sort of a healthful convalescence, for they certainly were no woodsmen. The actual work that they accomplished was of little consequence. With one exception, they were a taciturn bunch. They took little notice of us, and we didn't go out of our way to strike up any conversations with them. In all, they stayed two weeks, then left as suddenly as they had arrived. Heinrich volunteered no explanation for their presence, and we were not sufficiently curious to ask any questions.

One of the four was quite friendly and would come over and exchange a few words every once in a while. Max had been a butcher's helper in a Hoboken grocery for fifteen years, returning to Germany in 1936. A heavyset man, he had apparently broken his nose many years before, and it had been improperly set. Max looked like an inept preliminary bout fighter who had finished his last dozen bouts with his back on the canvas. He was eager to talk about Hoboken, and it was amusing to hear a real Al Smith accent in the Pomeranian forests.

Splitting cordwood one morning, Jess McDonald and I were startled by a loud crashing noise overhead. It sounded like some large object floundering through the branches. We shouted to Heinrich, who was a hundred feet away, convulsed with laughter. "It is a *Vogel* [bird], a *Vogel,*" he roared between peals of laughter.

Jess stared at him in disbelief and murmured, "It must have been a bloody winged elephant." We were sure old Heinrich couldn't be serious with this "bird" story. After he recovered his composure, he came over and started to explain, but every time he looked at our faces he started to laugh again. Finally he said it was a *"Kinder Bringer"* (bringer of children), and then we got it and joined in the laughter. By this time the rest of the boys had wandered over to see what all the commotion was about, and we told them about our first experience with a stork. A day or so later there we heard another stork, and this time we had a good look at the ponderous white bird, wings flailing away, seemingly staying aloft by the grace of God and sheer willpower. Heinrich told us that while they were not plentiful, they were native to this area, and the legends about stork association with childbirth had its origin in Pomerania. He seemed surprised to learn that it was a story widely told to children in the U.S.

I am convinced that a battalion of paratroopers, equipment and all, could have landed with less uproar than this single stork cruising, or rather battering, his way through the pine forest.

CHAPTER 17

Farewell, Benzin

Returning from the woods late one afternoon, we beheld a strange sight. The normally lifeless road on which all Benzin fronted was jammed with a procession of the most unique vehicles imaginable. It looked for the entire world like a second-rate movie version of a covered wagon train on the last lap of the Oregon Trail. There were dozens of ramshackle farm wagons, each with a hooped framework or canopy arrangement lashed down with canvas, tarpaulin, or even stitched-together burlap potato sacking. Some of the wagons were drawn by fairly decent-looking teams, but between the shafts of the majority were the most bedraggled horseflesh seen outside of a glue factory. Poor old nags, their ribs jutted out in bold relief with hip bones projecting like jug handles. Some were actually asleep between the shafts. These wagons at the head of the column were the cream of the crop. Farther back, the rigs were even worse, with some drawn by oxen, and one or two even had cows harnessed up.

The spiritless procession, a good fifty wagons, creaked along at a slow walking pace. Household effects and, once in a while, wan children's faces could be seen in the exposed rear of the wagons.

As we approached the main farm, we saw the *Inspektor* shouting at a stranger from the caravan. The *Inspektor* was hopping mad, there was no doubt about that. He kept roaring, "No, no, you will have to go on, there's no room for you here." By the side of the road was a wagon with a broken axle. The smith, Paul Mahn, and Franz Mahn were lashing up some kind

140

of emergency repairs to allow the decrepit wagon to limp along a few more kilometers.

This was the first of many such caravans that streamed through Benzin from January 20 to February 16. Thousands of similar groups must have been passing along hundreds of Pomeranian side roads. These people were called *Flüchtlings* (refugees), and although the native Germans professed deep sympathy for the poor wretches, I never saw them actually do anything to help them. Of course, the Mahn brothers did fix the broken axle that first day, but that was prompted not so much by sympathy as by a desire to be sure that Benzin was not saddled with a family of human derelicts. I think one reason for the rather callous attitude of the Benzin residents was that these people—most of them at any rate—were not of German stock. They were Ukrainians, Lithuanians, Estonians, and a sprinkling of Germans from Courland and East Prussia. They had been on the roads for many weeks. Though their equipment may have been presentable when they started, it was falling apart by the time they hit Benzin.

We were able to talk to a few of these refugees one Sunday as a large caravan paused to water their horses. The Russian advance had been so swift that many of them had only enough time to throw the barest of necessities into a farm cart, leaving behind furnishings and treasured possessions representing years of accumulation. They told of bucking heavy snows through Prussia, of horses dying in harness of exhaustion and malnutrition, of unharnessing the carcasses and putting cows between the shafts, of hundreds of wagons falling out of the mass trek with the tides of war swirling over the derelict wagons, and of family units being divided among more fortunate fellow travelers whose wagons were still able to travel a few more kilometers. As the horses weakened, the wagons were lightened, and there was a trail of debris stretching back to the starting point.

The men's faces were somber as they thought of fertile acres, barns, farmhouses, and tractors to which they knew they would never return. God alone knew how many hundreds of

miles more they must attempt to travel before finding a sanctuary. Though the roads were covered with deep snow, grandmothers and tots alike struggled along on foot behind the
wagon to ease the burden of the horse, or ox, on whom all
depended. Only the sick—and there were many of these—had
the luxury of a jolting ride.

They were a broken, dispirited people. Farms, homes,
herds, crops—all swept up in the holocaust of total war. The
chilly reception they were getting from the Pomeranians must
have been salt in their wounds. The *Wehrmacht* had com-
pounded their problems by insisting they keep to the secondary roads to leave the fairly well-paved main arteries open for
military traffic.

The only common factor tying this motley group together
was an all-pervading, hysterical fear of the "Russkies." I think
that all of them, except for the German East Prussians, had
found it expedient to switch to the conqueror's side in the
early tide of German victories. Because of that, they could not
dare to stay put and be "liberated" by the Russians.

There had been many turncoats back in 1941. Whole
brigades of Polish and Ukrainian troops had switched uniforms
and manned the battle lines against the Russians. Knowing the
Slavic temperament, we could well imagine the fate of such
"Judases" when their fellow townsmen sat in judgment on them.
No wonder they were a people apart, despised by the Germans
as outlanders and subhumans, yet understandably terrified of
the inevitable retribution they would face if they did not flee.
They were despised by both Germans and Russians.

However we might scorn the menfolk, we could not but
pity the children, their feet bundled up in rags, with wooden
shoes, or no shoes at all, noses dripping in the bitter cold. Most
nights they spent huddled in the wagon, except on those infrequent occasions when a farmer with some compassion would
permit them the use of a barn and the chance to snuggle down
between the warm bodies of cattle. The horses, grim carica-
tures that they were, had an equally gloomy fate in store. They
would live another week, another month, and then would lay

down their burden forever. In their pitiable condition, they might have looked forward to death. On and on this stark exodus trudged along Benzin's lone cobbled road.

The refugees were proof positive "Uncle Joe" Stalin was roaring toward Benzin, and by all outward indications could be expected by March 1 or even sooner. Our morale soared, though we were careful not to give outward indication of our elation to the Germans. We all had too much at stake to adopt a cocky attitude at this stage of the game.

I was fairly pleased with my culinary progress in 1944. In November I had developed a rye pancake, which was different at any rate. On January 22, my second civilian food parcel arrived. Another bonanza of delicacies: a can of pork and beans, some sardines, canned tuna, more Jell-O, and a can of peaches. During this period, I engaged in some research with Chester Stough. We were experimenting with making ice cream from powdered milk, water, and finely powdered D bar chocolate. The tests were not especially successful, but the resulting mess was palatable, so the ingredients did not go to waste.

One afternoon in early February, I had my worst scare while at Benzin. The woods crew was plodding back to the barracks about a couple of hundred feet behind Hank Conlin, who was piloting his six-horse team back to the barn. Suddenly all hell broke loose. A lead horse slipped on the icy cobblestones and crashed to his knees. He screamed in pain as blood poured over the glazed cobblestones, and the other five horses reared up in fright. Harnessed to their fallen mate, two of the other horses went down. In an instant, the road was a mass of writhing, struggling, panic-stricken horseflesh, their hooves flailing out, kicking cobblestones and fellow horses indiscriminately.

Old Heinrich sized up the situation at a glance, and he and Conlin sprang into the turmoil to soothe the lead horses and get them back on their feet, if possible. With some urging, we woodsmen took over the lead horses while Heinrich and Hank steadied the second pair. Fortunately we were right in the center of the village, and in a minute or two there was a crowd of Jerries joining the fray. We had to give up any efforts to try to get the fallen horses up, and started concentrating on maintaining the status quo.

After about ten minutes, we brought order out of the chaos and, starting with the lead team, got the horses upright and unharnessed. Puffing and snorting, many bleeding, they were all jittery, but fortunately no bones were broken. We let them stand apart from each other for another ten minutes, and then carefully led them, single file, back to their stalls. Conlin, Pierce, and Henderson all stayed out in the stalls until seven o'clock, soothing them and swabbing and bandaging their cut legs. By some miracle, all of the men escaped the flying hooves unscathed. It was a terrifying experience to me, and I'm sure none of my GI buddies enjoyed it either.

On February 17, at about 6:00 P.M., the *Inspektor* came into the barracks and called me outside. Electrifying news: We were to pack all of our belongings and be ready to leave Benzin by ten o'clock the next morning. I tried to get further details, but he only knew that we were all to leave Benzin permanently and that our first stop would be Stolp. He had received a phone call from guard headquarters at Stolp only a half hour before coming over to see us.

The boys received the news with mixed emotions. We knew that it must be linked to the major Russian advance then in progress, but whether the move would be for better or for worse only time would tell. I immediately distributed the remainder of our Red Cross parcels, three per man, plus the remnants of the one we were now working on.

The *Inspektor* produced some binder twine, and in short order we had lashed all of our worldly possessions into shoulder packs. Some of the boys were fortunate enough to come across some harness straps and fashioned respectable packs. They wouldn't have passed any basic training sergeant's inspection, but at Benzin perfection was seldom attained.

At 9:30 on the morning of February 18, a large truck drew up in the farmyard, and we filed out of our barracks with all of our goods lashed to our backs. We took a long look at our home of the past ten months, for we were certain that whatever might lie ahead, we would never cast eyes on Benzin again.

A civilian was driving, and with him was a surly-looking guard brandishing a Schmeisser machine pistol. This was unusual, because automatic weapons were not normally carried by guards other than SS men. It was a good big truck, as it had to be to take twenty men complete with packs as well as Shorty. The guard who had come with the truck rode in the cab with the driver, leaving Shorty in back with the GIs.

We had quite a send-off. The crowd in the farmyard was amazing; all of Benzin, it seemed, had turned out to see us off. The German girls, the Uke maidens, the Frenchies, and numerous German *Hausfraus* (housewives) were clustered about the truck. The German field hands wished us well, and our friends the Frenchies were effusive as only Frenchmen can be. They carried on with emotional speeches and innumerable hand-shakes all around. Even the *Inspektor* gave us a genial wave of the hand as we lurched down the lane in low gear and swung onto the cobbled Stolp road.

We had certainly run the gamut of emotional experiences during our captivity. February 18 was a year to the day from our capitulation on the Anzio plain. It seemed an eternity.

Jack Dower and unidentified friend

POWs at Benzin, Pommern, Germany, 18 April 1944–19 February 1945. Standing (from left to right): Johnny DiCrecchio, Bill Walters, Ray Kudloski, Daniel Cardenas, Chester Stough, William Halvorsen, Daniel Henderson, Archie Blevins, and Delbert Kinder. Seated (from left to right): John Estock, John Benson, Jim Pierce, Harlynt Robinson, Jim McLean, Elmer Eagle, Hank Conlin, James Osak, Jesse McDonald, and Vernon Olson. Jack Dower is not pictured, as he was on a trip to the Red Cross depot.

The French POWs at Benzin

Dracena Avenue, Falmouth, Cornwall, England

Sylvia Thomas

PART THREE

The Trek Westward

CHAPTER 18

On the March

En route from Benzin to Stolp aboard the truck, there was much speculation about our future. Many thought that all the *Kommandos* were being recalled to *Stalag* II B in Hammerstein. Others thought we were merely being reassigned to some other farm or work area. All of us were keyed up with the tense expectancy that comes when dramatic changes are underway. Little did we know that we were off on the first leg of a foot trek across Germany, with ordeals ahead of us to match the tales of the *Flüchtlings*.

The truck rolled into the Stolp *Kaserne* and halted on the great drill field. Adjacent trucks were disgorging similar groups of GIs, revealing that this was a true mass movement of all prisoners in the entire Stolp area. Dismounting, we were ordered into a large armory structure, where we found that we were a minute part of a group of at least 2,000. About half of those on hand were GIs and the rest an assortment of British, Yugoslavs, and Canadians. There we stood, a little bewildered group in one corner of this monstrous shedlike building, while still more equally bewildered new arrivals came in through the giant double doors and milled about the floor.

There was no point in seeking information from the other GIs, who were as puzzled as we were. Spotting a wide-brimmed Aussie campaign hat, I angled over, pulled out my cigarettes, and quickly got the gist of the situation. The Aussies and several English and Canadian groups had been in *Stalags* and *Kommandos* in various areas of Poland, East Prussia, and Silesia. Many had been at a British *Stalag* at Thorn, Poland, and other sizeable groups had been at Lamsdorf and Marienburg. A few weeks earlier they had been uprooted, as we now were, and started off on a trek to the west.

At the eleventh hour, the *Wehrmacht* had seemingly made an abrupt decision that all Allied prisoners were to be kept out of Russian hands at all costs. For many men, the Russian artillery had been within earshot before they began to march. As they progressed, their ranks had swelled with additional groups, and on at least two occasions the column had grown so cumbersome as to be unmanageable and was split into separate groups. They had been at Stolp the past two days waiting for the prisoners in this area to be rounded up to join the column.

The British were firmly of the opinion that moving the prisoners had been a spontaneous decision, as there was no indication of any planning. The route had been circuitous so far, avoiding most major towns, and billeting arrangements were left up to the march commandant when it became too late in the day to press on. The guard complement was fairly large and changed frequently. Most were cyclists, with a jeep fore and aft of the column, both mounting machine guns, and either a truck or wagon bringing up the rear and collecting casualties.

A few minutes later, I spotted Jack Schick in the midst of a horde of GIs and got substantially the same story from him. We were to bed down in the armory that night and get off to an early start in the morning. Schick was cleaning out his remaining supplies, as there was little point in maintaining any stock with all the prisoners heading west on the high road. We secured several GI aluminum cups, canteens, and mess kits that last night at Stolp.

We slept that night under the huge vaulted steel girder roof of the armory, overcoats rolled up for pillows and packs at our sides. Our packs must have weighed about 45 to 50 pounds on the average, for they contained three full Red Cross parcels at 10 pounds each, a loaf of Benzin rye bread, the remains of our current week's parcel, a blanket, extra socks, perhaps a spare shirt, shaving gear, and a toothbrush. A few men had an extra pair of pants, but in general our clothing consisted of what we were wearing.

This Stolp halt had swelled the ranks of the marchers, and we newcomers were not above taking a tip from the more seasoned travelers. They told us that a day's march ran anywhere from twelve to fifteen miles, and for chaps out of practice, a 50-pound pack was a heavy burden. We appreciated the advice and spent some time that evening rearranging our goods, especially the shoulder straps, so the loads would ride as easily as possible.

This tremendous building, as large as a football field, was easily guarded, for there were only two giant pairs of double doors, one on each side, each big enough to drive a tank through. The Jerries merely posted half a dozen guards at each door, and we were securely boxed in.

Next morning we all set out in high spirits and for the first few hours found the brisk pace through entirely new terrain almost invigorating. Ten-minute halts were called hourly. Shortly after leaving the outskirts of Stolp, we had gone off on a small secondary road in accordance with the accepted practice of not cluttering up the major arteries, which were heavily trafficked with military convoys. The noontime halt was for forty-five minutes, time enough to prepare a sandwich and heat water for coffee by kindling a few pine twigs.

After lunch, the novelty of marching wore off, and before long we were all extremely conscious of the pack straps cutting into our shoulders. Our feet had had enough marching by now and started to ache. There was a light covering of snow on the stubbled fields, but the road surface was clear and dry and the day bright and sunny with a chill wind. Our little Benzin group bunched together, but as the day wore on two or three of the boys dropped back a few ranks, unable to match the brisk pace set by the head of the column. Mile after mile we trudged over little-used farm roads, always in the general direction of the now-setting sun.

Shortly before dusk, we halted in the road before a large farm while the ranking officer, a German major, arranged for our billeting with the farm overseer. As they both came out of the farmhouse, the major was gesticulating and pointing to some papers in his hand. These must have been documents empowering him to commandeer, at least temporarily, quarters for both marchers and guards. The civilian was none too happy about the matter, but knew better than to question military authority too vigorously. With a resigned gesture, he waved to a couple of large barns behind the house. The long column filed into the two designated barns and staked out claims in the straw. The guards gave us a long harangue about the absolute prohibition of fires of any kind and gave us a half hour to fill our canteens at the barnyard pump. We came out in groups of fifteen for this purpose. We were all pretty tuckered out, and with no light in the barn and the prospect of another grueling day on the morrow, we were soon asleep.

Up bright and early the next morning, I had a stroke of luck in finding a flat board, like a shingle, in the farmyard. I hacked off two thin flat strips with my jackknife. Securing them to the shoulders of my overcoat, I spread the weight of the pack over a much wider area so it didn't cut in at two focal points. The rest of the shingle and a bit of straw sufficed to heat up a cup of coffee.

We hit the road at seven o'clock, and by ten o'clock that morning were just outside a fair-sized town called Schlawe. We halted within sight of the church spires while the lead jeep went into town for routing instructions. Upon its return, we swung off on a fork in the road, bypassing the town to the north. To my surprise, the route continued northerly for the better part of the afternoon. I had a good concept of north Pomeranian geography and was convinced that if we held to our course much longer, we would strike the Baltic. Stolp, our starting point, was on the Stolp River, only about twenty-five miles inland from Stolpmünde (Mouth of the Stolp). Any pronounced deviation to the north, if long continued, must inevitably lead us to the sea.

After the noontime halt, the aching weariness set in again, and the last couple of miles were sheer agony. The only thing that gave us a measure of encouragement was the recollection that our first week of farm work at Benzin had been murder, but we had soon become inured to it. We only hoped that we would eventually get used to this damned marching. At this point, I seriously doubted I would survive the transition period.

About 3:00 P.M., a column of seventeen Canadians joined us from a side farm lane. They had been quartered down the road a couple of miles and told us we were heading for Rügenswalde, a fishing town and minor Baltic port about four miles ahead. At four o'clock, we crested a small ridge, and there spread before us, still a couple of miles away, was the dull, slate-gray Baltic. From the ridgetop we sniffed the salty, acrid sea breeze. In the distance, terns and gulls wheeled and swooped along the water's edge. This was my first glimpse of the sea since Anzio, fifteen months ago and some 1,200 miles to the south. Off to the left, along the shore, was a town, still too far away to make out many distinguishable features. A square church bell tower was etched against the purpling sky, surrounded by lower buildings.

We spent the night at a relatively small farm two kilometers from Rügenswalde. Turning in that night, I noted that my feet were badly swollen. Lots of the other boys were experiencing similar difficulties. During the last five miles, several of our Benzin crew had fallen back almost to the extreme rear rank of the column and were using most of the brief halt periods to make up some of the lost ground. This gave them a bit of a cushion, or head start, for the inevitable falling behind that was sure to occur again during the next stint of marching. The trailing "meat wagon" had about eight men aboard who were absolutely incapable of walking at all, along with a rotating lot of rear rank marchers. These boys were not entirely physically spent and would ride for about an hour, then get off to make room for some other poor devil worse off than themselves. As we massaged our aching feet that night, many of the marchers who had started this trip way back in Poland or Silesia cautioned that we would have a hell of a time getting our shoes back on in the morning. How right they were. It was their contention that in the circumstances, it was better to keep one's shoes on twenty-four hours a day. After the third day, we adopted this practice also.

Rügenswalde was a pretty town in the early morning mists. Neat stone jetties jutted out from the main road, which was a sort of roadway and pier combined. The road had a granite sea-wall on its right side, with houses and commercial buildings along the left side. Tied up, the gentle swell slapping their hulls, were many small trawlers and coastwise craft intermixed with several tiny one-man fishing boats. How frustrating to look at this array of vessels and calculate that across a relatively small body of water lay Sweden and blissful internment.

Once through Rügenswalde, we swung away from the water on a new tack to the southwest. There was a gradual rise for about a mile and a half as Rügenswalde fell away behind us, and it was here that the march began to exact its toll. Slumping down for our ten-minute break, a few of the boys began to discard some of the carefully husbanded articles from their packs in a desperate endeavor to lighten their load. Men threw jackets, spare pants, extra blankets, and a few pairs of extra shoes into the ditch alongside the road. We practically littered the next two-mile stretch with discarded articles. Once in a while, a boy would fall out and lie twitching by the roadside. A couple of sturdier buddies would get him up and try to get him going again by supporting him from each side. Sometimes it helped to take his pack for a mile while he got his wind back. Most of the time this proved but a temporary respite, and when he was too far gone he went into the meat wagon, at which time he dispossessed the most robust-looking of the riders.

With Rügenswalde a good twelve miles behind us, we called it quits for the day and spent the night at a very large farm where there was a group of at least twenty Frenchies. A few of us were fortunate enough to buy some eggs from one of the Frenchmen for a few cigarettes. We drank the eggs and they went down well. We had all long since finished the food from the open parcel we had started with and had made substantial inroads into the first of the three full parcels we were carrying.

We never conversed with the guards who, for the most part, rode slowly along the sides of the column on their bicycles. During the first day, we did exchange a few words during a ten-minute halt, but their answers were surly and taciturn, and by the second day we were too concerned with saving every ounce of energy to waste any effort on fruitless conversation. We never got to recognize any of the guards, and it was our opinion that a fresh group took over every second or third night.

After we passed Rügenswalde, a second meat wagon was added to the tail of the column. The old law of supply and demand was at work. As we passed through fair-sized towns with hospital facilities, the really bad cases—boys absolutely incapable of further walking—were dropped off at both military and civilian facilities. In this fashion, additional meat-wagon space was created for the next day's casualties.

It paid to keep well up near the head of the column so we could get a bit of rest during the ten-minute breaks. At times, the column would stretch out for three-quarters of a mile, with wide gaps in the wavering line of exhausted marchers. When this happened, the normal break would be doubled to twenty minutes while the entire guard complement cursed and shouted at the stragglers, using their rifle butts indiscriminately to close the gaps. The poor devils near the tail end forfeited the entire rest period as they made up lost ground.

The Benzin bunch got well shuffled around from the second day onward. Pierce, Henderson, Estock, and Olson kept up in front; DiCrecchio, Benson, McDonald, and I struggled desperately to hang in somewhere around the middle; and several of our boys brought up the rear. It was certain that at least three of our boys had caved in and were no longer in the column. Faces expressionless, only half-conscious of where we were, we stumbled along on this endless treadmill, feet trudging ahead robotically.

CHAPTER 19

Bonanza at Treptow

The English newspapers were describing the trek as a "Death March." As the Red Army pressed ever forward from the east, this wave of prisoners and deportees struggled inexorably to the west. Dimly, we all knew that this vacuum area between onrushing Russian and steadily advancing GI was daily decreasing in size. No one thought much about what would happen when we had traveled so far that we must meet the advancing Allies. It all seemed so remote. Our only concern was to struggle through each new day.

Heads bowed, we only had eyes for the back of the man in front. Our one impelling thought was to never let the space between us widen. It became an obsession, crowding out any other thoughts. We must concentrate every ounce of energy on maintaining the fixed ratio between our feet and the back of the man in front. Some men actually slept while marching; often when the column would halt, those behind would stumble blindly onward, only halting when they crashed into the man ahead.

As we progressed toward central Germany, the evidence of the terrible ravages wrought by Allied air strikes became more and more pronounced. Often while on the march, we saw gangs of conscripted civilians digging earthen trenches and erecting log barricades with freshly felled timbers. In our state of semiawareness, however, these sights failed to bring elation or even true comprehension. Fortunately, the terrain was practically as flat as at Benzin, so there were no grades to contend with.

From Rügenswalde, we veered to the southwest, passing slightly to the north of Koslin. A day or two later, we were on a northwest tack again, heading toward the Baltic port of Kolberg. Snow and rain fell on several days but never in sufficient quantity to affect us much other than to cut a mile or two off the normal quota. The one thing working in our favor was that as we made further inroads in our food supplies, our packs became less heavy. This was a mixed blessing, for God alone knew when we would have a chance to stock up again, if ever.

The second day out of Koslin, the column was split into two groups, and I and six others of the original Benzin bunch were part of the smaller party. It was an odd division because the split was nowhere near equal. The main body took a road fork going off to the south, while our group of about 250 prisoners followed the coastline into Kolberg. There was a great deal of confusion among our captors regarding routes and the splitting of the column, which was inexplicable.

I am now convinced that this indecision reflected the almost complete collapse of liaison and troop authority in the *Wehrmacht*. There was no doubt that the column leaders were playing it by ear, making their own on-the-spot decisions about routes and policy. It had been our belief all along that the entire mass movement came about as the result of a sudden decision on the part of the High Command. No doubt initial march orders had been given to the column commanders when they started the trek deep in Polish territory, but now the *Wehrmacht* seemed to have forgotten the prisoner migration, having many more vital things, like self-preservation, on their minds. If this analysis is correct—and in the light of later developments, I think it is—this meant that the prepared routes, guard change points, and other planning details had gone by the boards, and the column leaders were left to their own devices.

The one asset the march authorities had that still cut a lot of ice was a paper that gave them tremendous authority over civilians. This document was produced and flaunted every time barns were commandeered for sleeping quarters. On two or three instances, it was used to confiscate bread from bakeries in the large towns on our path. The bakers always put up a terrific howl, but when the magical paper was produced, they delivered the demanded number of loaves with alacrity. These bread rations about every third or fourth day were the only thing that kept the original marchers on their feet. We marveled at the stamina of those who had hung on all the way from Poland. We were well into our third and final Red Cross parcel by this time, and it would be just a matter of another two days before we also became entirely dependent on the occasional loaf of rye bread.

On the third day out of Kolberg, as we were nearing the town of Treptow, we got a real break. We were stretched out alongside the road taking one of our ten-minute rests, and my feet were in real bad shape by this time. I was well back in the rear ranks and wondering when I would cave in and end up in the meat wagon.

A couple of bereted Frenchies peered through the hedge by the roadside, quite agitated about something. They beckoned vigorously to me and a couple of the other boys, making sure that they were well screened from sight of the few guards who were now with us. My initial thought was that they wanted to trade something for cigarettes, and as I was down to only three or four, I knew that no deal could be consummated. I don't know what prompted me to hobble over to them, but I'm awfully glad I did. In a curious mixture of German, French, and English, they said that down a side road just a little way ahead was a depot of Red Cross parcels, under the supervision of a Swedish civilian, set up expressly for issue to nomadic bands of prisoners like ours. They wanted to be sure that we knew about it, as the road on which it was located was little more than a farm lane that we would certainly pass by if not specifically alerted. I remember them saying *"Croix Rouge, Croix Rouge"* over and over, their eyes big as half-dollars.

About three of us prisoners limped up to the head of the column, which was about ready to start up again, and informed the German lieutenant in charge about the Red Cross depot. He was a young fellow and had been with us only since the

major column split after Koslin. Looking at us in puzzlement as
our words literally tumbled out, he agreed to take a look. I had
the directions, and as it was just a matter of two kilometers, a
little more than a mile, the lieutenant, the driver, and I bundled into the jeep for a quick reconnaissance. The rest of the
marchers were left back by the roadside with a sergeant in
charge. As we drove along, I prayed that the information was
correct, as the lieutenant was sure to be sore as hell if it proved
to be a wild goose chase. But sure enough, about a half mile up
a rutted dirt road was a barn with a crude Red Cross sign
propped up in front.

As we drove up, a civilian emerged from the barn, obviously
the Swede in charge, for he had on a business suit, incongruous
garb for a farmer. He acknowledged that he was in charge of
issuing parcels and that stocks had been laid in especially for
cases such as this. He made quite a point of explaining that the
food was provided for the express use of the prisoners, plainly
inferring that he didn't propose to issue any to the Germans.
The lieutenant, a fairly nice chap, didn't seem too disconcerted
at this remark and was apparently genuinely pleased at our
good fortune. He stayed with me and sent the jeep driver back
to pilot in the rest of the column. The Swede spoke good
English, and from our short ride together, I knew that the lieutenant had no knowledge of English at all.

While waiting for the rest of the boys to join us, we all went
into the barn, where there must have been a thousand parcels
piled up. Talking to the Swede in English, I told him there were
approximately 250 in our group and that I doubted there
would be many passing this way from now on, as we were the tail
end of the march. Situated where he was, off the main road and
with no signs posted, it was probable that ours would be the last
request to be filled from his ample stocks. In consideration of
these facts, I felt he should issue two parcels each to the prisoners and treat the half-dozen German guards in similar fashion.

He was dead set against this latter suggestion, but I again
emphasized that he was in no danger of having his supply

depleted, and surely it was better to make a practical use of the parcels than have them go to waste. Further, the Germans had been pretty decent to take the trouble to investigate the Frenchies' tip. As they would be our custodians for some time to come, it would behoove us to stay on the right side of them. He pondered this for a few minutes, then agreed that the arguments I had marshaled had a lot of merit and that he would go along with the idea, even though it was a situation not covered by the book.

In a few minutes, the wavering column of marchers hove into sight and set up a roar of joy when they spotted the Red Cross sign. The Swede waited until the German lieutenant and the handful of guards were right in front of the barn, and then explained in fluent German that regulations called for issue only to prisoners. He had been advised, however, that the combatants had treated us fairly, and in consideration of this, he would also issue two parcels to each of the seven Germans. This was wringing all the psychological goodwill out of the situation that it could yield. The Germans positively beamed, and the lieutenant gave me a broad grin and wink. He, for one, was under no illusions as to who had instigated the deal.

In gratitude, the lieutenant held us over at the Red Cross depot farm for three wonderful days, while Germans and GIs alike had a real feast and time to rest. The Germans almost went mad over the Nescafé and the American cigarettes. Probably the most peculiar feature about the whole deal was that if the lieutenant had chosen to wave his pistol, he could easily have seized the entire parcel supply. Several times before, the dominant German soldiers had exercised unusual restraint when dealing with neutrals. Apparently the German soldier, whatever his attitude toward his own civilians and prisoners of war, stood in awe of alien civilians, especially Red Cross workers. Why this should have been the case I don't know, for there was no compelling reason why the Swedes or Swiss should have been treated any better than we were in those chaotic times. If the Swede had any parcels left when the Russians rolled through a few weeks later, I'm sure they would have had no compunctions about relieving him of his stock, with perhaps a lump on the head to boot.

On our second day at the farm, the lieutenant and I chiseled four parcels for the Frenchies who had steered us into this treasure trove. They were petrified when the German army jeep drove up in front of their quarters, but after our errand had been explained and the parcels passed around, they were happier about the situation than we were.

When we hit the road again, three days later, there was no doubt that our experiment in public relations had paid off. The halts were much more frequent. Morale is truly a wonderful thing, and for the first day or two we strode along with almost as much pep as we had on the fateful morning that we left the Stolp *Kaserne*.

By this time, there was ample evidence on all sides of the almost complete disintegration of civilian and military cohesion and authority. Crude tank ditches and timber roadblocks were being constructed on all roads of any importance, though German morale was now so low it was unlikely that anybody manned these primitive barricades when Uncle Joe's tanks and flamethrowers came wheeling through soon after.

One scene is etched in my mind with vivid clarity. Some eight miles out of Treptow, on the coastal road to Kammin, there was a crossroad dominated by a gigantic beech tree. Hanging from a limb on this tree, so low his boots were only slightly higher than head level, was a young German in civilian clothes, a *Wehrmacht* helmet on his head. On his chest a lettered sign read: THIS IS THE FATE THAT AWAITS THOSE WHO DESERT THE FATHERLAND. By this time, it was common knowledge that wholesale desertions were taking place in all branches of the German armed forces, and here was firsthand proof of the violence of the countermeasures. In passing, we skirted the base of the tree, giving the grim corpse a wide berth.

In a similar vein, we passed a company of infantry being marched, under actual duress, up to the front. There must have been about a hundred in the group, all old graybeards or youngsters of fifteen or sixteen. Most likely they were all brand-new conscripts. The body of men was preceded, flanked, and followed by a dozen SS troops, all with Schmeissers in firing position. There was no doubt about it: These infantry troops were more truly prisoners than we were. It was ironic to see the envious glances cast at our sorry crew heading the other direction, away from the holocaust. The last three rows of marchers were actually blubbering as they plodded eastward to probable extinction. This was a far cry from the proud *Wehrmacht* of a year ago that had strutted along singing "We're Marching on England," "Horst Wessel Lied," and other boastful military airs. The Third Reich had certainly been a firm believer in the morale-boosting effect of martial music.

That the Russians were close behind was no great secret. On some nights, from our barn quarters, we could see a distant red flickering in the eastern sky and, if the wind was right, sometimes we could hear the muted crump of far-off artillery fire. Peculiarly, we saw no Russian planes in the skies, or *Luftwaffe* either, for that matter. The few civilians we saw were grim-faced, men, women, and children alike. This was the homestretch, and everybody knew it. It would take a dozen miracles to salvage the war now. There was only one unspoken question: How much longer before they throw in the sponge?

CHAPTER 20

Dumped in the Meat Wagon

On the day we approached the old town of Kammin, my feet gave out completely. For some days they had been badly swollen, and eventually they began to bleed and could no longer take my sustained weight. The pace had stepped up tremendously during the past few days, and the meat wagon was operating at full capacity. I passed out on the roadside about three miles short of the outskirts of Kammin. Johnny DiCrecchio dropped out of the march the same day.

I woke up a day or two later in a wooden barracks with four other GIs, a Canadian, and a Scot. They told me I had been dumped in the meat wagon and that eighteen of us had been left that night just short of Kammin in a little woods camp with two guards. It appeared that our friendly overtures at the Red Cross depot had borne fruit, for the lieutenant had found us a nice billet and had sent back a dozen loaves of rye bread for us before continuing the march with the bulk of the column.

The next day, I was able to get up and move about a little. We were in a wooded glen, housed in three log cabin–type structures. All told, there were six of these cabins in a semi-circle. The buildings were most unusual for German construction, of split logs with the bark left on the outer surfaces and rustic full-length porches. They were the type of cabin one associated with the Adirondacks, ski trails, or Boy Scout camps. The camp had previously housed some small troop detachment, perhaps an ack-ack crew that had pulled up stakes. Our guards didn't bother us much, just came in two or three times a day for a quick head count. Actually they had no need to take elaborate precautions, as none of us could do more than hobble about. We still had almost a full Red Cross parcel each and the bread worked out to two-thirds of a loaf apiece, so we were not badly off for food.

The important thing was to get our feet back into shape again. We were able to borrow an axe from the guards and cut a lot of kindling. In addition, we got a few handfuls of salt. There was a large wooden tub in the barracks, and we would fill it with scalding water, add the salt, and sitting in a circle, soak our feet for hours on end. This helped a great deal. In a couple of days, we were able, once again, to walk without too much difficulty.

Toward dusk on the fourth day of the rather placid existence at our forest sanctuary, heavy cannonading broke out not too far to our rear. A major Russian breakthrough was in the works. It was no surprise when our two guards came dashing into the barracks a few minutes later shouting *"Raus! Raus! Schnell!"* We were to take to the roads again, this time with the Russians virtually at our heels. Of the eighteen of us, fifteen were assessed fit enough to resume marching. The other three were to go only a mile into the village and be left with the civil authorities there, in the town jail, I believe, which sounded like a nice safe place. In ten minutes we were well on our way, our three badly off buddies supported by the strongest of the fifteen marchers.

This would be a night march, and unless I missed my guess, an all-night march. A cold, chilling rain was lashing down as we shuffled along the deserted cobbled streets of Kammin. Not a light showed in the town, and the stone buildings towered over the narrow streets like ghostly sentinels wreathed in fog. We paused for about five minutes while the three casualties were bundled through a doorway, and then we were off again.

As the River Oder passes Stettin, it widens out to form a large bay or gulf. Two large islands almost seal off this body of water from the main waters of the Baltic. The first island from the east bank town of Kammin is Wollin, a triangle of land some twenty miles in length on its longest side. We were to cover the entire length that night along the only surfaced road that bisected the island in its northern sector. Such a march in pouring rain would have been a man-sized assignment for a well-conditioned detachment of garrison troops. It was sheer torture for a miserable lot of exhausted, undernourished prisoners, but somehow, mainly on willpower, we made it.

As we were leaving Kammin over the long stone bridge crossing the Oder, we saw our first signs of activity that night. About a dozen German *Pioniere* (military engineers) were busily stringing wire along the bridge abutments. They were working swiftly by the light of electric torches. We had gone no more than a mile and a half when we heard—and felt—a series of mighty explosions. The bridge had been demolished. Looking back, we saw the sky over Kammin was livid. We were the last people to pass over the only bridge for many miles down the Oder.

We later learned that the bulk of the civilians in Kammin had crossed the bridge an hour before we came through the town, which accounted for the virtual desertion of the place when we arrived. The civilians had swung south down the road to the village of Wollin, while we had taken the road due west that bisected the long axis of the island and led to the city of Swinemünde.

Mile after mile we slogged along, meeting no one, seeing no one, struggling to keep up with the tremendous pace our bicycle-riding guards were setting. The rain came down with renewed fury, sometimes turning to icy sleet. Wollin Island was a peculiar place. We saw no houses of any kind, just dense woods crowding in on the road from each side. The only light came from an often-obscured sliver of pale moon and the bobbing headlamps of the guards' two bicycles. Bleak, inhospitable Wollin Island: Well were we to remember that night.

Now that the bridge was blown up behind us, I felt reasonably secure and could not account for the blistering pace. The guards were still reasonably friendly, so after about seven miles, I asked why we were pushing so hard. The guard said there was no shelter at all along this road and we might as well push on full speed for Swinemünde, where there would surely be a barn for such a small group. We were in no position to protest, so there was nothing to do but keep moving as quickly as we could. The temperature had dropped, and during those interminable small hours of the morning the rain was freezing as it struck, making walking all the more difficult.

The moon was now completely clouded over, and in the pitch blackness the only light was from the bobbing lights of our guards, one up ahead and one at the rear. Fifteen automatons, limbs numb, kept moving forward, conscious only of the fact that we must reach Swinemünde or perish in the attempt.

About four o'clock, even the guards realized we were out on our feet, so they gave us about thirty minutes to muster up enough strength to continue. We were all sound asleep before we hit the frozen roadside. All too soon, we felt the prodding of a boot or rifle butt. We blinked our eyes open to find the rain had ceased and the first pearly gray light was visible in the eastern sky. Ahead it was still black and somber, and the dense woods encroaching on our road were dripping from the night's downpour. We were all filled with an overpowering reluctance to struggle to our feet. Once we were up again, the column lurched forward once more. At last, a dim sun cut through the veil, and roadside objects became distinguishable. The terrain was dismal and sodden, but as time passed, we emerged from the densely forested area and came to stubbled fields. We were approaching human habitation again. Finally we saw a few huddled figures up ahead, clustered near an army jeep sitting in a field. We were shepherded into the field to join this group of prisoners. Physically spent, we pitched forward to the ground, packs still strapped to our backs, and were oblivious of everything in a matter of minutes.

When we awoke, it was early afternoon. The sun was a dim lackluster sphere in the gray sky, and the chill of the frozen earth on which we had lain had permeated our very bones. Our clothing, drenched during the night's march, was still soggy and being further chilled by cold gusts of wind sweeping in from the Baltic. Around us were some hundred GIs and

Tommies who had crossed onto the island at the village of Wollin and had made the cross-island trek two days before, along the southerly road.

Everybody was scrounging for sticks and twigs in this god-forsaken, forlorn field. The few bits of wood that we did find were so saturated they resisted all efforts to get a fire going. Clothes soaking wet, teeth chattering, we huddled in disconsolate little groups, flailing our arms about, hopping up and down, doing anything to generate a little circulation to fight off the all-pervading chill.

Finally a dispirited, smoldering fire took hold, and we threw on all the limbs and twigs we had gathered to make one good blaze. Everybody swarmed around the fire. Once they had warmed up, the men in the inner circle made way for the ones on the outer perimeter. As our clothing dried, our spirits improved.

Joining a new group of prisoners always inspired conversation. This new lot included two very colorful prisoners: a chap called Frank Hardmeyer from Albany, New York, and another man from Greenwich, Connecticut, whose name eludes me. Both of them had been American volunteers in the ill-fated Lincoln Brigade during the Spanish Civil War.

During the late afternoon, the jeep made several trips, and each time it returned, the German guards conferred. Probably they were discussing our future route and the progress of the Russian troops, who had been right on our tail back at Kammin. Our complement of guards was now eight: one captain, one sergeant, and six privates. All of the guards had a lot of heavy thinking to do these days, wondering what the fate of their homes and families was and trying to make a personal equation out of this dying convulsion that was choking the Third Reich.

We had no way of gauging the German resistance at this time, but to us it hardly seemed likely that the Russians had as yet cut us off. Assuming that the only other bridge to Wollin Island, that at the village of Wollin, had been blown up like the bridge at Kammin, it meant that the Russians would have to have covered two sides of the triangle to beat us to

Swinemünde. If this had been the case, we were quite sure there would have been a lot more panic and that the boys who arrived two days ago would have already been moved out.

During the early evening, we learned that we were three kilometers east of the port city of Swinemünde and that the Russians were being held, at least temporarily, on the east bank of the Oder. As the evening wore on with no announcement from the guards, it became apparent that we were fated to spend still another Spartan night camping in this dismal field. We were just about at the end of our parcel food, but we scraped up enough to make a fair supper before bundling in our blankets for another night under the stars.

Early the next morning the guards came around, shouting that we were to prepare to move out very soon. Leaving the field with no regrets, we soon were approaching Swinemünde, a fair-sized place straddling the mouth of the Swine River. The bulk of the town was on the west bank, but there was quite a group of houses, warehouses, and commercial buildings on the eastern shore. In particular, there was a long line of low barracks in a row along the main road, housing a very large group of Frenchies. The column paused in the road opposite the French barracks while the jeep made a quick trip up the road for further instructions. It gave us a chance to talk to some of the Frenchmen through the barbed wire. They were stevedores and freight handlers on the Swinemünde docks.

Swinemünde was quite different from any other place we had seen along the line of march. For one thing, it was a busy port facility, and in addition, large bodies of army troops and naval personnel were garrisoned there. At least two U-boats were anchored in the roads, and against the offshore haze we could make out several surface craft of destroyer size and larger. Along the docks and quays were a number of merchant vessels. The streets were filled with sailors and soldiers and, as in sailors' towns the world over, a full complement of heavily made-up streetwalkers.

Passing through the main part of the town and going off on a southwesterly tangent, we received a bread ration in an assembly-line technique. The entire column filed into the front door of a bakery and kept going out the back door into an alley and back onto the route of march. As he walked through the bakery, each man was given a loaf of rye bread. The method got the bread issued in a hurry without impeding the forward progress of the column.

Once out of Swinemünde, the countryside was pleasant. The plentiful farms had a prosperous, tidy look, with well-maintained outbuildings and fertile fields. By noon, the sun came out and it developed into a fairly nice day, though cool.

The next city ahead, barring hamlets, was Anklam, but it was several days away at our rate of progress. The pace was now much more moderate. Whether this was in consideration of our grueling quick march across Wollin Island, the fact that we had a little breathing room between us and the oncoming Russians, or for some other reason, we did not know. We were grateful for any respite, however slight, and for that reason had no desire to inquire into our good fortune. That night we bedded down in a large farm building just off the main road. We had been on the march a little more than four weeks and had put a large part of eastern Germany behind us.

The next day our pace was equally moderate, and after ten miles we turned down a dirt road to a cluster of farm buildings. These were small outbuildings, so we split up into several parties for the night. The farmer and his wife actually seemed pleased to have us quartered there.

In the morning, we were told that we would stay over here another day and that there would be a soup issue. We selected four or five boys to help prepare the meal. The *Hausfrau* provided several large iron pots and tripods and a veritable mountain of potatoes. Once the fires were lit, the spuds peeled, and the water boiling, the woman returned with some carrots and turnips. This was an unexpected bonus.

The warmth of our reception the night before at this particular farm had surprised us. Most places, after considerable wrangling, gave us grudging shelter on the strength of the army warrant.

We were now all allowed considerable latitude, as there were relatively few guards, and these seemed to have weighty problems of their own. There were no head counts, and in this particular place, quartered in several small buildings, it would have been easy to slip away. Frankly, I don't think our captors would have been especially perturbed if a couple of us had taken French leave.

From snatches of conversation with Poles and Frenchmen en route, we knew that the area now under control of the Germans was shrinking like a snowball on a July day. They were rapidly being compressed into the northwest quadrant of the country. The Russians were at the gates of Stettin, the Americans were racing from the Saar across central Germany, and the British and Canadians were slicing through Holland, headed for the base of the Danish peninsula.

All of us had analyzed our position, and it would have been foolhardy to take major risks when, by sitting tight and sweating it out another few weeks at the most, we were almost certain to be delivered. The guards, though laconic and introspective, seemed friendlier than at any time since leaving Stolp. This could have meant that with the table soon to be reversed they did not want to be turned over to the Allies and accused of brutalities or undue harshness.

On the second morning, we were again heading toward Anklam. About three o'clock that afternoon electrifying news came sweeping back from the head of the column: There was a Red Cross parcel depot only about a mile up the road! Sure enough, after we went on a few hundred yards, a large Red Cross insignia and an arrow indicated that the distribution point was only a kilometer and a half up the road. This was extremely timely, for we had run out of food completely at Swinemünde and since that time had subsisted solely on the loaf of rye bread and the soup issue of the previous morning. It had looked as if we would be tightening our belts with a vengeance in the days to come.

This Red Cross depot was manned by two civilians, a Swiss and a Swede. Well-marked and located on a major road, the depot had doled out thousands of parcels over the past few weeks. Although the supplies were low, they were ample for our hundred-man group. As each man passed in single file, he was given a parcel. We noted that about a dozen parcels were put into the captain's jeep. We were all in favor of this, for it was to our advantage to have our captors in as good a mood as possible.

Both Hardmeyer and I asked the Swiss to provide a double parcel issue, but he demurred, pointing out that we were en route to Neubrandenburg, only a four-day march away, where there were ample stocks. This was very encouraging news and had the flair of authenticity that stories from objective parties possess. We agreed it seemed foolish to carry an extra 10 pounds on our backs. If plenty of parcels were waiting for us—and we had no reason to doubt him—it would be carrying coals to Newcastle to cart an extra box for nothing. With light hearts and blistered feet, we peeled off another couple of miles to our resting place that night, a farm some two miles outside of Anklam.

DiCrecchio, Hardmeyer, and I were huddled around a small pile of blazing straw in the farmyard that evening, brewing up a pot of Nescafé, when an elderly German wandered over and struck up a conversation in excellent English. This was quite a surprise. Though many Germans knew some basic English, this was the first one we had met, apart from a few army clerks and interpreters, who really spoke our language fluently.

The old Jerry—he must have been seventy—told us that in his younger days he had sailed around the world many times, bringing back animal collections for the Hamburg Zoo. It was his contention that during the 1920s the Hamburg Zoo boasted the finest wild animal collection in captivity. He was acquainted with the States and had been commissioned to supply many birds, snakes, and other animals for the Philadelphia Zoo. Reminiscing, the old man told us he had been in charge of safari and hunting arrangements for Kaiser Wilhelm, who had been an enthusiastic sportsman.

The old man went into the house for a few minutes, then returned with a metal box full of photographs and yellowed newspaper clippings. One clipping, under a Sao Paulo dateline, showed the Kaiser, Teddy Roosevelt, and our newfound friend, each carrying huge Mannlicher hunting rifles, standing over a slain antelope. We all enjoyed talking with the old gentleman.

We hit the straw that night in excellent spirits. We had a full Red Cross parcel, we were now fairly accustomed to the marching, the war news continued to be excellent, and we were only four days removed from Neubrandenburg, where additional parcels awaited.

The old man was up early the next morning, straight as a ramrod, to shake hands with us as we filed out onto the highway again. I remember well his parting words: "*Deutschland* is *kaputt* [done for]. You know it—I know it. Perhaps it is as well. But mark my words, and mark them well: The greatest menace to mankind lies to the east. Someday—I won't see it, but you will—Americans, English, and Germans must march as comrades in arms to wipe out Bolshevism, or perish themselves through lack of foresight and common purpose."

CHAPTER 21

Stalag III B, Neubrandenburg

When we passed through Swinemünde, we had left Pomerania behind and entered the province of Mecklenburg. Up to this point, there had been no marked difference in terrain. Now we encountered some gradual rises, too small to be termed hills, yet a departure from the billiard-table topography to which we had been so long accustomed. The farms were smaller, one-man holdings, and the area more densely populated.

The column bypassed Anklam on the south. Twice we pulled off on the shoulders of the road to make way for military convoys headed eastward. On our second day past Anklam, we saw firsthand evidence of the chaos that Allied air strikes had wrought upon an already overburdened railway system. There was a small hamlet grouped around a railroad switching point where two major rail lines converged. Approaching, even in the distance, we saw a jam of goods trains far beyond the normal capacity of a fairly small junction point. Going on farther, we saw gaping craters and twisted rails for hundreds of yards. Entire trains had been systematically riddled with machine-gun fire. Many carriages had been overturned, others were still standing, but all were immobilized. Gangs of women and children were making frantic, futile efforts to clear one track.

Later that afternoon, a great armada of Allied planes passed overhead, silvered wings gleaming in the late March sunlight. A few dispirited puffs of black ack-ack went up, but it was apparent to all that the *Luftwaffe* had ceased to exist as a fighting force and that the Allies could roam the German skies at will, picking their targets with precision and delivering hammer blows. We needed no urging from the guards to disperse and hit the dirt until the flight passed onward. It would be tragic indeed to cash in our chips now, after all of the obstacles we had overcome, and doubly ironic if it were at the hands of our comrades in arms.

Four days out of Anklam, we entered the city of Neubrandenburg, a pretty place, the sort of gingerbread, medieval fortress town that railway posters glory in. The narrow streets were flanked with four- and five-storied gabled and turreted buildings, all linked together and displaying half-timbered construction. Every few hundred yards, the cobbled street would be bridged by stone arches linking quaint towers with tiny mullion-paned window slits. Neubrandenburg must have been one of those peacetime tourist meccas that capitalized on its quaintness. In many ways it seemed a university town, for the cobbled streets were lined with bookstores, art galleries, and gift shops. In the middle of the city was a huge park, complete with swan pools, botanical gardens, and much statuary. Passing alongside the park, we climbed a long, steep hill. This was a real test. We were all gasping for breath long before we were halfway to the summit.

Shortly before reaching the crest, we saw the familiar diagonally striped guardhouse and the striped wooden cross arm blocking the roadway. Barbed wire stretched away from each side of the road, and guardhouse, searchlight, and gun towers reared skyward at the corners of the enclosure. We had arrived at *Stalag* III B, Neubrandenburg.

The camp was a small one by *Stalag* VII A and even *Stalag* II B standards, and unlike either was right on the fringe of a good-sized city. Checking in, we had the luxury of a good hot shower and the usual delousing.

It was a wonderful experience to let the scalding suds cut through the grime and sweat picked up during five weeks of marching and sleeping in our stinking clothes, and to know that we had reached the relative sanctuary of a *Stalag*. With little ceremony, we were herded into the barracks, and in a few minutes most of the camp had come around to meet the new arrivals.

DiCrecchio and I were delighted to meet up with four of our former Benzin comrades. The original column had split up several times since Johnny and I fell out before Kammin, and no one knew where the others were.

We were quartered in a barracks next door to a group of British paratroopers, survivors of the ill-fated airborne assault on Arnhem. This was the first time we had seen the distinctive red berets of the paratroopers, as the British we had met at Moosburg, in Italy, and on the march were all ground troops captured in the African desert, or else veterans of the original British Expeditionary Force who had missed the last boats from Dunkirk way back in the spring of 1940.

These paratroopers were a young, vigorous lot who could scarcely credit the amazing exploits of their countrymen in hoofing it all the way from the middle of Poland on essentially starvation rations. They soon were passing around mugs of tea and plying us with questions. Actually, there was little that we could tell them that they didn't already know, but they were able to give us a lot of information concerning our new surroundings.

The camp had been primarily British until January, when a sizeable contingent of Americans taken during the Battle of the Bulge had been sent there. It had stayed about half British and half American until late February, when a group of Canadian Dieppe survivors had arrived on foot from *Stalag* XII A at Stargard in Pomerania. For the past two weeks, several small columns like ours had swelled the *Stalag* III B complement, these for the most part mixed-nationality groups.

The camp, though severe in their eyes, was well run and amply stocked with Red Cross food. Issuing day was Saturday, and men were permitted a hot shower weekly. The barracks were in fairly good condition and not as closely quartered as any of the previous camps I had been in. After tramping across half of Germany, it was a glorious feeling to be able to take off our shoes and luxuriate, flat on our backs, in the straw-filled bunks.

We had checked in on a Thursday afternoon, and Friday was a day of true relaxation, no marching in store, nothing to do but cruise aimlessly through the barracks, chatting and exchanging stories with prisoners from many lands. Hardmeyer, DiCrecchio, and I stayed together for the most part. Frank was especially at home with the Canadians, as he had volunteered in the Canadian forces in early 1940, but transferred back to the U.S. Army in England after we entered the war. I too always felt a little more affinity for the Canadians than the British, or other Dominion troops, as we had more or less a common heritage and interests.

These Dieppe Canadians were a really fine bunch of fellows. All told of the handcuffing edict handed down by the prison camp authorities at Lamsdorf in 1943, when all of the Canadians were handcuffed in retaliation for some alleged incident involving German prisoners taken at Dieppe, the abortive initial major landing effort in France. Practically all of them had fashioned tiny wooden handcuffs, about watch fob size, as souvenirs and a grim reminder of the hardships encountered during their earlier days of enforced exile in Germany.

At noon there was a soup issue, the familiar potatoes and cabbage. It was steaming hot and went down well. We had long since abandoned whatever gourmet notions we might have once had. Any solid staple food really hit the spot. Tomorrow would be parcel issue day.

Rumors swept through the camp. The most credible one was that Neubrandenburg, so far unscathed, was not to be defended. The entire *Stalag* personnel, together with the thousands of other prisoners now compressed in the rapidly diminishing Third Reich, were to be evacuated up through Schleswig-Holstein into Denmark, where the *Wehrmacht* and SS were to dig in and make a final, fanatic stand.

Friday afternoon, DiCrecchio came rushing into the barracks with the news that Nick D'Errico was in the *Stalag Lazarette* in a bad way, his feet battered to a pulp. Nick was the New Haven boy who had gone through basic training with us in Spartanburg, South Carolina, and later traveled with us through North Africa until we were separated at Bizerte. We hadn't seen him since leaving Hammerstein, about a year ago, and even at that time his feet, frostbitten in Italy, were giving him a lot of grief. He evaded *Kommando* duty because of his feet and by virtue of membership in the *Stalag* band.

The *Lazarette* was large in relation to the fairly small camp population, but this was accounted for by the fact that the great bulk of the patients were not inmates of long standing, but marchers who had caved in en route. These had been dropped off at various small towns by the meat wagons. A truck convoy had come along, picking up these isolated detachments and bringing them on to *Stalag* III B for medical attention.

Nick was genuinely pleased to see us. He had been there about two weeks, and his feet, though extremely painful, were improving. From Nick, we had an account of the mass migration as it affected *Stalag* II B, Hammerstein. They had taken off about the same time that we had, but pursued a more southerly course. Nick had been able to go along only for a week before his feet, frozen at Montecassino, had given out completely, and he was put in a small hospital at Tempelburg with four other GIs. After a couple of weeks he was sent to Stettin, then a couple of weeks ago reshipped to Neubrandenburg.

Saturday dawned, clear and bright. From our location atop the ridge, we could look down right into the center of Neubrandenburg. Truly it was a picture-book town. Parcels were issued at 10:30 A.M., and the 1:00 P.M. soup issue was supplemented by a few golf ball–size spuds. By now we had learned the hard way never to spurn food, no matter how unappetizing it might look.

These barracks differed from the conventional single-room type at *Stalag* VII A and *Stalag* II B in that they were partitioned off into six equal-sized rooms, three on each side of the central corridor that linked the front and rear exits. Each room was about fifteen feet square, and we were quartered twelve to a room. In our room, besides Johnny and me, were three other GIs, four Canadians, and three British. The Canadians were a lively crew, one from Lethbridge, two from the Toronto area, and a Montrealer.

For the next four days, we got back into the routine of *Stalag* life once again. The camp library was well stocked, and a couple of the barracks even boasted a wind-up record player. Daily we stopped in to see D'Errico, who continued to improve, though it was evident that it would be a long, long time before he would be able to walk, unaided, again.

On Thursday, a week after our arrival, we were told that half the camp was to move out the following morning. Johnny and I were both in the group chosen to move. Camp authorities rushed through an emergency parcel issue, two per man, that night. Next morning, packed and ready to leave, we were each given a half loaf of rye bread. We had just enough time for a hasty handshake with Nick before the column filed out the main gate and down the slope into Neubrandenburg proper. Just before reaching the main part of town, we swung off to the left and halted alongside a railway spur track on which was drawn up a long string of boxcars.

The fact that it was to be a train ride left us with mixed emotions. Make no mistake about it, we had all had our fill of tramping on foot through the German countryside, but the German rolling stock had been taking a terrific pasting from the skies of late. We were all visibly encouraged when we saw the large Red Crosses on a white field painted on the top surfaces of the boxcars. There was no guarantee, but we could hope that the American Air Force and the RAF were granting immunity to trains so marked. Of course, this was a privilege the Germans could well abuse, and knowing them as well as we did, there was little doubt in our minds that thousands of tons of war materials must have been moved in similarly marked cars. One thing was certain: It wouldn't be a very long ride. There wasn't much of Germany left anymore.

We milled about the siding for most of the day, finding that the U.S. Army had no monopoly on the "hurry up and wait" principle. I was not too unhappy about the delay. Any train rides that might have to be made these days were much better undertaken under cover of night, the blacker the better. Finally, about 3:30 P.M., we clambered aboard and were soon under way.

It was the Moosburg to Stolp ride all over again: the same nail keg privy, the same drafty pitch-black boxcar, though this time we were not wedged in quite so tightly. A few of us had jackknives, and with a little work on the car walls, we soon created a couple of fair-sized peepholes.

Once during the night, the car jolted to a halt. In a second, we were all wide awake and climbing over each other for a peek out the closest peephole. We were in a large railhead town where sets of tracks converged from many directions. In the starry night, yellow lanterns bobbed as the train inched its way between rows of idle locomotives and carriages. This yard had received a good going-over from the air not too long ago, for splintered cars lay toppled on their sides amid tracks bent and twisted like so many strands of spaghetti. Great gaping bomb craters flanked the one or two lines still usable. There was apparently only one major line that had been hastily patched up and put in working order, and we were threading our way along this route with frequent switchings and halts. This was no situation to inspire confidence, especially on a night as bright as this one. We all prayed inwardly that the train might soon work its way out of this hellhole and pick up speed in open country.

In the clear, frosty night, the station sign's Gothic script was plainly legible as we inched past a murky waiting room. It was Schwerin, a large industrial center not too far east of Hamburg. We had really covered ground since pulling out of Neubrandenburg.

After some forty-five minutes of backing and filling, we had worked our way through this tangled mass of debris and were back on the main line again, peeling off kilometers at a good rate. Concerned as we were with the hazards of north German train rides in early April 1945, we knew there was no practical way of controlling our fate. With these fatalistic thoughts and the awareness that we might well be in for some hefty marching in the morning, I lapsed back into a fitful slumber.

Some hours later, the train ground to a halt again. We all woke up when they hit the brakes, as the entire passenger list slid forward to the front part of the car, to the chagrin and cursing of the rightful owners of that floor space. We had a couple of minutes for a quick look out the peephole and saw we were in open country fields and the dawn was upon us.

In a matter of minutes, the car door was unbolted and swung back, and we tumbled out to form ranks on the cinder roadbed. We needed no urging from the Jerries, as we were all eager to put lots of distance between ourselves and the prime target represented by the standing train.

Soon we were on the march again, across the fields and through the hedge onto a country road. This was a pleasant pastoral country, just beginning to burst into life with the full fervor of early spring. How strange that nature's seasons took their appointed course oblivious of the insignificant brawling of multinational strife.

Filled with two full Red Cross parcels, our packs were now heavier than at any time since leaving Stolp, and by noontime we were all pretty well tuckered out. We turned off the surfaced road into a wooded glen and rested for almost an hour, taking advantage of the halt to knock down a couple of man-sized sandwiches.

At two o'clock, we circled to the south of a large city, which a guard identified as Lüneburg. Now we were poised at the base of the Danish peninsula. This gave further credence to the rumor, so widely accepted at *Stalag* III B, that we were to be sent north into Denmark. We had just been chased out of the east, we couldn't go much farther west without bumping into Montgomery, and the southern perimeter was daily being driven in by Bradley, Patton, and the rest. What could be more logical than a swing to the north?

All afternoon, as we walked beyond Lüneburg, we saw repeated massed flights of Allied planes soaring overhead. The *Luftwaffe* was nowhere to be seen. The planes passed out of sight to the northeast, probably to give Lübeck or Rostock a thorough pummeling. About four miles past Lüneburg we turned in for the night at another mammoth collective farm.

CHAPTER 22

Stalag X B, Sandbostel

The next two days were uneventful, just more marching and still more glimpses of American bombers overhead. Each time we heard the drone of far-off massed engines, we fanned out into the fields. As long as we were dispersed and passing through rural areas, we felt no real alarm, as these missions were doubtless aimed at major industrial or shipping targets. The thing that might have worried us was fighter planes out for a strafing, but as luck would have it, we saw none of these.

On the afternoon of our third day out of Lüneburg, we had our first real close-up look at the ghastly, pitiful plight of concentration camp inmates. Passing a large barbed enclosure, we saw a column of emaciated living dead men shambling out through the gates, herded by a squad of SS men. Our two columns were abreast, going in opposite directions, and we were almost close enough to reach out and touch these poor devils, so close and yet so far. Protruding eyeballs dominated hawklike parchment faces. They stared at us beseechingly. All were in strange pajama-type outfits, broad blue or purple stripes on a dirty white or gray background. They wore little square caps of the same material, with wooden clogs or strips of auto tire casings strapped to their feet. This was a sight to put to shame the wildest imaginings of Dante: men seemingly back from the grave, slavering madmen, a sight almost beyond human comprehension.

Overcome with pity, most of our boys tried to toss a bit of bread, some prunes, anything, to these walking skeletons. To our alarm, they set upon each other like wild men. Mouths working and foaming, croaking unintelligible sounds, they clawed at each other. An SS man stared at us, and then fired a burst close over our heads and theirs. Three or four other SS troopers rushed up and, swinging rifle butts in crunching arcs, restored some semblance of order. Down our column came the cry, "Stop, you're not being kind to the poor devils, just making it worse for them." It was true. As much as we wanted to help, it was clear we were only making the lot of these miserable souls worse. Three or four of them lay prostrate, blood running down their faces. They staggered up again, apparently insensible to pain.

The dreaded SS troops swung their weapons at our boys in menacing fashion. It was a touch-and-go situation, and any ill-advised move could precipitate a bloody massacre. Our guards were panic-stricken, as afraid of the SS boys as we were.

As we passed on, we could see through the open gates a long line of small hand railway hopper cars, such as are used on construction jobs to haul cement, heaped with corpses, all in faded striped outfits. It was several miles before our tensed nerves relaxed. The memory of that forlorn column stayed with me long after I had quitted Germany. What were their crimes? That they were non-Aryans, or perhaps a few who had the temerity to question some of the policies laid down by the Führer. I swear most of them weighed less than 70 pounds.

Toward noontime the next day, we entered an area of scrub pine, and by 1:30 P.M. the familiar outlines of a *Stalag* appeared on the western horizon. This was *Stalag* X B, Sandbostel. Once more we had arrived at a temporary home. Sandbostel lay on a sandy plain about forty miles north-northeast of Bremen and about fifty miles west of Hamburg. Like *Stalag* III B in Neubrandenburg, it was a relatively small camp and only filled to half-capacity when we arrived. Most of those already there were British, and all of these were fairly recent arrivals, including the remnants of the original marchers from Prussia and Poland. It had the same cement barracks, the same guard towers and sentry boxes—the same drab scenery. The only thing about Sandbostel that surpassed anything previous was the smell of its latrine building. We had thought that La Torina and Moosburg excelled in this field, but we were in for a shock. The Sandbostel stench defied all human comprehension. The nauseating fumes swirled over the camp, and to actually enter the building called for all the moral courage any of us could summon up.

The deterioration in German morale, first noticeable when we left Stolp, had become progressively more pronounced as we moved farther west. The surveillance had been casual enough at III B, but here at Sandbostel it was almost perfunctory. Of course the guard towers were manned night and day, but the crispness was gone from the Jerry commands. The occasional head count, though God knows what figure they tried to tally with, was pretty much a case of just going through the motions.

The original occupants of Sandbostel, those displaced to make room for us evacuees, had apparently been predominantly British. This we gleaned from the addresses, limericks, and scribblings on the barracks walls. Names of vessels had been written in many instances, indicating that at least some of them had been seamen.

While at Sandbostel, I met two of the most unusual prisoners ever taken by the *Wehrmacht,* though the Germans themselves were unaware of it. In our room was an old army sergeant who for many years had been stationed in peacetime army posts at San Antonio. He was of Mexican extraction and a native of El Paso. One day he was conversing in rapid-fire Spanish with two other GIs who, by their features and coloring, were also apparently of Mexican stock. I thought little of the incident, though it was unusual to hear a language other than English spoken in the barracks.

After a few minutes, the sergeant brought the two over to me and translated as they related the strangest story I had ever heard. The boys were Argentinian nationals and petrified lest that fact become known to the Germans, for to the best of our knowledge, Argentina was still ostensibly at peace with Germany. One of these men was called Sanchez; I have forgotten the name of the other.

These men, idealists and of good parentage, had volunteered with the Loyalist forces during the Spanish Civil War in 1936 and had fought in the bloody battles of the Ebro River and the outskirts of Barcelona. With the collapse of the Loyalist forces, they had fled Spain and made their way across to North Africa, joining up with Marshall Weygand's French Foreign Legion to continue their two-man crusade against fascism. As Weygand hemmed and hawed in 1940 and finally, in taking no decisive action, became a Vichyite by default, they pulled stakes and deserted from the Legion. In the face of seemingly insuperable obstacles, they made their way across all of North Africa to Cairo and continued to Syria, where they joined up with the Free French forces of General Juin. The Syrian area became a quiet stalemate. Bored with the inactivity there, they again disassociated themselves and trekked back to Egypt, joining a mixed group of Commonwealth troops then sailing from Alexandria to defend Crete. Here they got a full measure of the combat that they had traveled thousands of miles to find. In bitter fighting at Heraklion, with the New Zealanders under General Freyberg, they were captured.

The whole story was utterly fantastic, but in all fairness I had no real reason to disbelieve them, as they were both quiet, modest men, and to have spun such a wild tale for my benefit would have been pointless. I was frankly skeptical at the manner in which they joined various armies with apparent ease and a complete lack of any documentation. They replied that the French Foreign Legion routinely turns a blind eye to enlistees' backgrounds. When they reached Juin, and later the British, the need for fighting men was so acute that screening was dispensed with. After their capture in Crete, there was no interrogation, at least of privates, and they were accepted as Commonwealth troops. This was understandable, as the term "Commonwealth troops" covers an awful lot of ground. Jamaicans, Sikhs, Ghurkas, Maoris, Maltese, Cypriots, and dozens of other national groups fell into this loose classification.

Sanchez, via the interpreting sergeant, added that when the question of their national origin arose later at a German transit camp, they professed to be natives of British Honduras. This well-considered story explained their fluency in Spanish and their rudimentary knowledge of English in one swoop. Of course, I don't think any troops ever were actually raised in British Honduras, but the Germans could hardly disprove such a contention. It was possible. At the time of their capture at Crete, with the Axis at its zenith and prisoners pouring into Third Reich stockades by the thousands, I'm sure the Germans were not about to devote a lot of research into the origin of two mere privates.

During the march from Poland the two Argentines had, in the interests of expediency, become GIs simply by picking up spare GI clothing discarded by weary marchers. It was a weird tale, but the boys quietly and satisfactorily answered the variety of questions that both the sergeant and I posed to them. At the outset, we were frankly very dubious of their story, but in the end both of us were convinced their statements were authentic. Both the sergeant and I pledged to keep their secret and assured them that there seemed little danger such a fantastic hoax, which had been carried on for six years on three continents, should now be exposed in the waning moments of the war.

Later that day, the sergeant explained how the strange conversation had begun. Being an "Old Army" sergeant, a garrison and drill field soldier, he had been brought up in an era of white-glove inspections and taught to observe—and enforce—rigid cleanliness of equipment and uniforms. Although most of us stayed reasonably clean, these boys had made a ritual of cleanliness. With amazement, the sergeant daily noticed these two rigorously polishing buttons and shoes until they positively gleamed. Noting the Latin cast to their features, he had tossed a remark to them in Spanish and they had responded in kind. Even then, he was by no means prepared for such a bizarre story, as his initial impression was that they were, like himself, of Mexican stock from south Texas, or perhaps Southern California. It was only after a few minutes of preliminary conversation that they told him their story.

With their permission, the sergeant confided in me with the positive assurance that it would go no further. It must have been a wonderful experience for these two lads to have found someone with whom they could converse in their native tongue, after years of captivity with Scots and Lancashiremen. I don't suppose their limited English caused too much suspicion among the British, as they had stuck to their Honduras story. Even the British sometimes had difficulty understanding each other, as within the relatively narrow confines of the UK there was an amazing variety of brogues and dialects. The Scots were the prime offenders in this regard. Many times I had seen New Zealanders, Welshmen, and Cornishmen stare in bewildered amazement when a Scot or Geordie had some tale to tell, especially if he was excited.

In the following days, I often looked in on Sanchez and his buddy and nodded a greeting. Both the sergeant and I respected their confidence and were discreet, for the last thing the boys wanted was to be objects of curiosity. Once in a while, the four of us would go off to some quiet area outside the barracks, well away from the others, to have a quiet chat. During such talks, with the sergeant doing a yeoman's job as interpreter, they divulged that they had become devotees of button and shoe polishing during their tenure with the Foreign Legion, where such spit and polish is considered the hallmark of a good soldier. The habit was well ingrained, and today they are probably two of the most immaculately groomed men in Buenos Aires.

All told, we were at Sandbostel for six days.

CHAPTER 23

Marlag und Milag Nord

On April 6, and again on April 7, large groups were marched out of Sandbostel. On the following day, the remainder of the camp hit the road again. This was one time it paid to be in the last group, for when we cleaned out the camp parcel stock there were enough Red Cross parcels for two per man.

We started off in a westerly direction, but just three miles out of the gates, our group was split and forty of us were marched off to the south. Once again there seemed no sensible reason for breaking into divergent columns, especially with one group of over 300 and our little band of 40. Then again, it was nearly mid-April 1945, and many strange things were going on in Germany during those perilous days.

I had taken it for granted that we would head north into the Danish peninsula, so it was a great surprise to find us now trudging toward Bremen. As it turned out, it was only a one-day march. Just before sunset, the familiar silhouette of *Stalag* guard towers loomed on the horizon. Dusk was upon us as we were herded through the gates and past the striped "Sentinel Louie" guardhouse. This was *Marlag und Milag Nord* at Westertimke, some thirty miles almost due north of Bremen.

As soon as we were within the enclosure, we realized that although this place externally looked like the POW camps we had occupied, in a variety of ways this camp was very different. For one thing, until the arrival of our forty soldiers, it had been an encampment solely for captured naval personnel and some civilian internees. Actually, there were two separate detached compounds, one for Royal Navy men and the other, in which we were quartered, set aside for Merchant Navy prisoners and a scattering of civilian internees. *Marlag* stands for *Marine Lager*, or naval camp. *Milag* stands for *Marineinterniertenlager*, or marine internment camp. *Nord* means north.

As we circulated around the camp the next morning, many other equally strange departures from *Stalag* life as we knew it became obvious. All of us were immediately impressed with the cleanliness of the camp. A cluster of neat barracks somewhat detached from the main group was actually flanked by flowerbeds and ornamental shrubbery. There was a cricket field and a building set aside for amateur theatricals, complete with stage and seating. By our standards, this was really living.

The neat barracks were occupied by captains, chief engineers, mates, and others of high rank, some having batmen. They were nicely quartered, two to a room, and some of the real top brass had rooms to themselves. This was a strange concept to us, for in the army *Stalags* there were only a very few officers who served as administrators and chaplains. Most captured army officers were maintained in entirely separate camps called *Oflags*.

That morning, we had ample opportunities to talk with a great many of the sailor prisoners, virtually all of whom were British. We were all greatly impressed with the scrupulous regard given to rank by these mariners, particularly the Royal Navy men. Our army lads, once captured, still had a measure of respect for officers, but saluting was a thing of the past, and we would have had no hesitation in striking up a casual conversation without regard for formality or protocol. Here at *Marlag und Milag Nord*, it was entirely different. Much deference and respect was shown those of rank by all hands, and there were clearly defined layers of social strata within the wire. Let me say that this was not due to any flaunting of authority by the officers, but rather was an instinctive perpetuation of long-ingrained habits of discipline on the part of the seamen.

The most important difference between *Marlag und Milag Nord* and any comparable *Stalag* lay in the fact that each separate branch of the German services served as the custodians of their own opposite numbers. The *Luftwaffe* ran the *Luft Stalags* for captured airmen, the *Wehrmacht* ran the army *Stalags*, and the German navy ran *Marlag und Milag Nord*. The German navy camp reflected the navy's sharply contrasting attitude toward prisoners of war. Bear three things in mind. First, the German navy—and this is admittedly a generalization—was made up of a much more cultured and gentlemanly element than the German army. Second, a noticeable affinity existed between the sailors of the German navy and the Royal Navy. The men shared a common respect for the technical knowledge and abilities of their counterparts, especially engineers, navigators, and radio men, whose chosen vocations made for a common interest. There was no such bond among army people. Third, while the *Wehrmacht* had to run hundreds of camps confining well over a million prisoners, the navy had only one camp, *Marlag und Milag Nord*, to operate.

The merchant seamen were very kindly and pleasant to us and greatly interested in our accounts of army *Stalag* life, particularly our recently concluded cross-Germany trek. We army boys were in that enviable position always accorded a minority group in such instances. We were the novelty of the hour at *Marlag und Milag Nord*, and the sailors went way out of their way to be obliging. I happen to be Cornish by birth, and when this became known, a host of Cornishmen came over to introduce themselves. In this group were Charlie Knuckey of Penryn, Bill Veal of St. Ives, Lee Iresidder of Falmouth, and Jim Jones from Truro.

Another Cornish expatriate, Bill Thomas, brought me around to the officers' quarters to meet the chief engineers, captains, and first officers. Bill was a man some twenty years my senior who had operated a travel agency in Brooklyn for many years. When the war began, motivated by a sense of patriotism and adventure, coupled with the high wages paid on merchant runs, Bill had signed on as a purser for one trip. Also, his mother was in England, which was being severely bombed at the time, and he took a calculated risk for a chance to see her. This was to have been a single trip, but a well-aimed torpedo made it a longer trip than Bill had ever contemplated when he signed on.

Many of these captured officers were making a tidy week's pay while languishing in prison. Most of the steamship companies continued their pay during their captivity, and for a first officer or captain, this was a hefty sum. As they had no conceivable way to spend it, the money was accruing to their accounts and drawing interest. In many cases, officers who were prisoners of long standing had built up a tidy nest egg, enough to buy a pub when all the shooting was over.

The living accommodations in this officers' section were luxurious by our standards, a far cry from the grime, austerity, and squalor of any *Stalag*. They had chairs, tables, and cots, some even a rug or carpet. The captains, with a batman to make the occasional pot of tea, had almost all the amenities of home.

In general, these men were more relaxed and much more conversationally inclined than soldiers. Perhaps this is accountable, in great measure, to the fact that most of them were intimately acquainted with the colorful nooks and crannies of the world, and they were almost without exception good storytellers. They could go on for hours, especially when they got onto such burning topics as turbines, knots per hour, fuel consumption, monsoons, relative seaworthiness of vessels they had served on, and other shop talk.

There seems to be a bond of fraternity and comradeship among seagoing men not duplicated in any other walk of life. Of course, there was a multitude of differences between these sailors and the soldiers. The average age of these men was at least thirty, contrasted with an average of no more than twenty-two for the soldiers. Also, where the typical GI was a draftee soldiering on a temporary basis, these sailors, for the most part, were career men pursuing their chosen life's work.

Down in the Royal Navy compound, the rank situation was even more pronounced. It was almost like the old poem, "Where the Cabots speak only to Lowells, and the Lowells speak only to God." Here were quartered naval officers and heroes whose names and deeds are now legend in British annals. These men had witnessed the scuttling of the *Graf Spee*, the Dieppe assault, the Dunkirk evacuation, and the heroic withdrawals of tattered remnants at Narvik, Andalsnes, Leros, and Suda Bay. Without exception, all had the utmost respect for the foot soldier of any nation who could carry on the grim business of warfare, day in and day out, on the front lines.

In keeping with navy traditions many—even the very young—were bearded. The most confusing situation, to me at least, was the engineers, all Scots and seemingly all answering either to Jock or Alec. The technical abilities of these men were staggering. They had fashioned several homemade radio receivers, and every night the BBC broadcasts were taken down verbatim, in shorthand, and transcribed. Twenty minutes after the broadcast signoff, printed news sheets were circulated through the barracks. To cite an example, President Roosevelt died on April 12. Complete details appeared in the camp newspaper on April 13, together with some background data on Harry Truman.

The entire operation provided for any eventuality. An elaborate set of warning signals was set up, and at the first sign of prowling guards, the entire apparatus could be dismantled and secreted away in a matter of seconds. Multiple receiving points were set up so that when a rig might be out of action temporarily, a standby set in another barracks was taking down the news.

This news operation was phenomenal. I honestly could not credit such a masterpiece of organization and planning until I had seen it for myself.

Hundreds of ships were represented at the *Marlag*, some with only one or two survivors, others with almost an entire ship's complement. Some had been sunk by U-boats, others by aerial bombardment, others in naval surface-craft engagements or by fire from shore batteries. Many of these men had drifted in the open sea in rafts or lifejackets for days, or even weeks, before being picked up.

Most of the sinkings had been between 1940 and 1943. The imposing roster of vessels represented included *City of Benares, Port Hobart,* HMS *Afridi, Rio Claro, Orama, Zam-Zam,* and the

Rawalpindi. The locations of the sinkings girdled the seven seas, from the Indian Ocean to the Falklands, the West African coast, the fjords of Norway, the Dodecanese Islands, and the icy Arctic waters of the bleak Murmansk convoy run.

On the third day after my arrival, I met a very soft-spoken man, a Reverend Russell, who had been a survivor from the sunken Egyptian vessel *Zam-Zam* in the early days of the war. Russell was an American missionary en route to his appointed station when the vicissitudes of war had abruptly altered the course of his life. He had heard that I was from Hartford, Connecticut, and as he had received his training at the Hartford Theological Seminary, we had a common interest.

I always felt very sorry for the civilian internees, notwithstanding the fact that they were treated relatively well, certainly much better than any military prisoners. The only parallel that comes to mind might be a situation where a racing car spins off the track, killing the driver and also taking the lives of some spectators. In such an instance, I would feel much greater compassion for the spectators because, after all, the driver had by his knowing participation in a dangerous sport been the means of his own destruction, while the bystanders were innocent victims of circumstance. This is probably not a very good analogy, as most of the GIs had been draftees, yet it was my conviction that the civilian internee had been treated more cruelly by fate than the imprisoned former combatant. Capture, to a soldier, must be considered an occupational hazard.

Prior to our arrival, there had been a goodly number of internees at *Milag*, but now there were but a few. Such well-known individuals as novelist P. G. Wodehouse and the British actor Henry Mollison had known the confines of the camp. Now, in addition to Reverend Russell, there were only a couple of British businessmen and a team of music hall jugglers. The jugglers had been arrested at a Berlin cabaret and observed that their captors at least had the good manners to allow them to complete their act before arresting them as they returned to their dressing rooms.

My pal Charlie Knuckey was very conversant with the internees' situation, as he had been confined with them in northern France for a long period. He told of the so-called "family camp," where entire family units were housed in separate quarters, mother, father, daughters, etc. It was surprising to learn how many there had been in this category, as it was my recollection that the signs of war were very clear back in 1939, and these people had plenty of time to get back to England. This was especially true of the large group of British internees from the south of France. These expatriates, for the most part, were successful businessmen, with a good sprinkling of authors, artists, and poets. They lived in France primarily for its climate and particularly to escape the severe British income taxes. In some sort of blind optimism, they had hung on long after the fate of France was sealed, perhaps in the belief that a peace settlement would be in the offing with the fall of Paris and the collapse of French resistance. By the time they realized the war was in dead earnest, avenues of escape to England or neutral countries had been sealed. Neither we, nor the sailors, felt any common bond with these internees, most of whom wound up in this plight as a result of their own damn foolishness. Of course, this was not the case with Russell and a few of the others, whose capture had been a caprice of fate.

In my barracks at *Milag Nord* was a group of Canadian survivors from the sunken HCMS *Athabaskan*. They were a friendly bunch, and surprisingly were mainly from Manitoba and Saskatchewan rather than the Maritime Provinces, where you would expect sailors to hail from. Another Canadian I recall was the oddly named Captain Kidd, a Montrealer whose room boasted as fine a collection of pin-up pictures as there was in Europe. He whiled away much of his spare time in correspondence with movie queens and had an impressive collection of autographed photos. Mae West was his favorite.

By April 20, the crumbling of the Third Reich was roaring to an agonized crescendo. The Americans were crossing into Czechoslovakia, the Russians were at the very gates of Berlin, and the British were driving north just short of Bremen.

Another three weeks, at the outside, and it surely must all be over. The German guards were staying pretty much in their own quarters now, and a large party of them left the camp on April 25. Spring was in its full glory in the surrounding countryside. The end was so obviously imminent that an extra parcel issue was made on April 26.

CHAPTER 24

Deliverance

April 27 was the day of an impressive ceremony. We knew that Bremen had fallen the day before and that the leading elements of the Second Army were within twenty miles of us at that very moment. Early in the morning, we were all formed into ranks on the large drill field immediately before the camp administration building. The German naval commander and the ranking British officer saluted each other at the base of the flagpole from which flew the red, white, and black German flag. A bugle call, tremulous and clear, rang out as the German, with much pomp and ceremony, handed his saber to the Briton. In the hush that followed, the English commander gravely offered up a short prayer of deliverance, then admonished us all to act with restraint and common sense until contact was made with the onrushing British troops. We were all to remain within the camp confines until the British forces arrived, which we expected would be within twenty-four hours. The German flag was lowered from the staff, folded, and handed to the former camp commandant. A tremendous cheer erupted as the White Ensign rose in its place and waved over *Marlag und Milag Nord* that fateful April 27. On the second flagpole the Red Ensign of the Royal Navy was unfurled.

For the past two weeks, swarms of Allied planes had passed overhead daily, many swooping to low altitude to take a close look at our camp. We were certain they knew our exact location. I don't think anyone went to bed that night. I know I didn't.

During the early hours of April 28, three Welsh Guards, faces blackened, crawled up and snipped through the perimeter wire of the *Marlag*. They hadn't realized the nature of the camp and were startled when a horde of shouting, cheering prisoners came rushing up to meet them and hustled them off to the office of the British camp commandant. They reported virtually no resistance other than some sniping by a few bands of fanatic Hitler Youth groups. At noontime on April 28, two Cromwell tanks rolled through the main gates in advance of lorried infantry. It was indeed all over.

Jubilant, we celebrated all afternoon and evening, wandering from barracks to barracks laughing, singing, giving full vent to long pent-up emotion in every possible way. I know we all pictured ourselves walking in our front doors and embracing our loved ones. We were feeling an overwhelming exhilaration that words just cannot possibly convey. Many of us were in tears. Few got much sleep again that night. This was the night we had dreamed of, some for as long as five full years.

This buoyant euphoria continued the next morning, but at noon a tragic incident occurred. I know that all of us with any sensibility had the sobering thought, *There but for the grace of God go I.*

I was crossing the parade ground quadrangle when I heard the keening whistle of an incoming mortar shell. It's a sound that once heard is never forgotten. In a split second, I was on my face, head cradled in my forearms, sprawled on the dusty ground. The shell sailed overhead, landing a couple of hundred yards away in the Royal Navy compound. It exploded with the characteristic *crump*. There was just the single shell.

As soon as I heard the impact explosion, I raced into the nearest barracks and huddled against the outside wall in the direction from which the shell had come. Cautiously, I stayed put a full fifteen minutes. Finally satisfied that the firing was over, I went out into the open to see a crowd of Royal Navy men thronged around one of the end barracks. From their actions and the bustle of activity, it was obvious there had been casualties. A half hour later we had the full story. Some poor devil, sunk in the summer of 1940, had been sitting with back to the barracks wall in the bright sunlight, writing a happy letter to his wife and kiddies. He had been killed by massive chest and abdominal wounds. By sheer good fortune, his buddies had been inside. Though some shrapnel had gone through a window, the brunt of it was absorbed by the cement barracks wall. One sailor had been hit, and he was dead.

This was such a poignant episode. Poor bugger, he had struggled through five years of privation, and now, after he had been liberated and was within a very few days of going home to his wife and family for a joyous reunion, some crazy Hitler Youth bastard had done this senseless thing.

CHAPTER 25

Further Travels of a RAMP

The next day, British army lorries started to evacuate us to Diepholz, where a special camp had been set up solely to collect, process, and pass along liberated prisoners. I think it took three days to move the entire camp. I was in the group that left *Marlag und Milag Nord* on the second day, April 30.

The lorries took us about ninety miles to a camp just outside the small town of Diepholz, some fifty miles south-southwest of Bremen. In circling around Bremen, we got a close-up look at the vicious pasting meted out by Allied bombers. Whole city blocks were just piles of bricks. A dusty pallor seemed to hang over the blighted city as a watery sun glinted down on solitary chimneys, heaped-up railcars, and crazily twisted tracks. Peculiarly, this vista of brutal retaliation, however rightful and deserved, did not give me the inner elation I had thought it might.

Once past the Bremen suburbs, the countryside turned pastoral again. Rolling along meandering secondary roads, we passed only military traffic. These were mostly jeeps scurrying along impatiently. We were occasionally halted at MP-manned roadblocks and checkpoints.

The shadows were starting to lengthen as we rolled into the Diepholz camp. Someone with a keen sense of the dramatic had laid this out. After jumping off the trucks and hobbling about to get the kinks out of our legs, we were brought to a large reception tent. Six strikingly attractive British, Australian, Canadian, and New Zealand NAAFI girls (Navy, Army, and Air

Force Institutes, the British equivalent of the USO) presided over heaping trays of sandwiches and buns, as well as steaming urns of tea, coffee, and, of all things, hot chocolate. Reclining wicker chairs were spread about for us to relax in and enjoy this leisurely feast. This was country club living, man.

Stuffed with fine food and drink, we stared at the NAAFI girls in sheer amazement. Remember, our German and Uke female associates had been on the plain side. Cosmetics, short skirts, lipstick, and nylons were unknown items in Pomerania. Now we were surrounded by a bevy of beauties who would have rated a second or even a third look in Hollywood. And talk about personality! If we tended to be shy, and most of us did, they would start the ball rolling with an offer of a sandwich, and soon we would be prattling away about our hometown or any other topic that came to mind.

Laid out in neat rows, all converging on the refreshment and social center tent, were scores of wooden-floored, eight-man pyramidal tents. In them were piled stacks of white wool navy blankets. There was plenty of room, and we were allowed to select our own tent. Generally, we seemed to wind up about four men per tent.

This camp was under the supervision of the Royal Navy, and that meant there was a daily issue of rum. Every afternoon the rum dispenser would halt outside each tent and loudly inquire how many men were inside. He would then pour into a tin cup as many shots of white rum as the response indicated, up to a maximum of eight, of course. It was strange how all of the tents occupied by three or four men miraculously became full eight-man tents at ration time. The rum was fiery hot. A single shot was enough to have me gasping. A second or two later, it created a warm glow within and an overall feeling of well-being.

During my three days at Diepholz, I learned I was now officially a member of a rather esoterically named group: RAMPs, an acronym for Recovered Allied Military Personnel. I suppose our theme song might have been "We are poor little RAMPs who have lost our way, baa, baa, baa."

On May 3, which was, appropriately enough, my birthday, the small band of Americans at Diepholz was trucked seventy miles in a convoy of six British Bedford lorries to Hannover. It was another lovely May day, and we were rolling along through an extremely attractive wooded region. It had only been a few days since these villages and hamlets had been liberated. On every hand were clear and conclusive signs of total collapse. Germany was truly *KAPUT.* Often we went by great log roadblocks, laboriously built then seemingly never defended. I suppose the might of the onward rushing Allied armies must have struck terror into the hearts of the small groups of Hitler Youth and graybeards pressed into service in the final, agonizing weeks.

Each cluster of crossroads buildings had bedsheets draped from every window, the universal "I give up" message. Once in a while we would go through a village where there were some indications of limited street fighting, but these spots were few and far between. Normally there would have been quite a few farmers out tilling these fertile-looking fields, but today there were virtually no civilians about. It was prudent, I guess, to stay indoors by the hearth these days.

We climbed out at a military airstrip a few miles west of the city of Hannover. The British had a system whereby combat fliers, after completing a certain number of missions, earned a few days off from active duty. Characteristically, we found that these South African and British bomber pilots unanimously volunteered to spend these "rest and relaxation earned days" flying us RAMPs out to Belgium and France.

Talk about your "no-frills" flights. We were loaded into Lancaster bombers, sitting on heaped blankets on the aluminum-ribbed inside decking where the bomb loads were usually stored. There were no chairs, benches, or windows, just a couple of handholds and a few canvas slop buckets, which came into use before we landed. Most of us had never flown before. By the standards of today, this was a really primitive way to start.

When the plane was climbing, we all had a tendency to slide backward, toward the tail. When we were coming down, we clung desperately to hooks, bolt heads, or whatever there was to grab to avoid piling up in a heap of humanity against the cockpit door.

I guess we must have taken off about two o'clock. I don't suppose the flight could have taken more than an hour, if that. We landed at another improvised airfield just outside the ancient Belgian city of Louvain. A windsock was flying in front of the airfield Quonset hut, and directly across the street was an enormous brickyard. Trucks were waiting to bring us about fifteen miles into downtown Brussels. While there were signs of damage along the way, it was sporadic, not the concentrated devastation seen in Bremen and environs.

Brussels was a dream come true. We were quartered two to a room in what had been a girls' school dormitory. It was in the heart of Brussels, only a few doors away from Allied Military Government headquarters. This was absolute bliss. We redis-covered cots, mattresses, sheets, pillowcases, and—luxury of luxuries—piping-hot water to shave with. We RAMPs were treated like visiting royalty. Issued mess kits, we filed into a cafe-teria-style mess hall for a delicious hot meal.

The next step was to give us each two telegram blanks so we could let the folks back home know we were hale and hearty, back in Allied hands, and on our way home. There was some limitation on the number of words per cable, but it was ample for me. As I was writing out my message to my mother, my mind turned for a brief couple of minutes to the poor seaman killed that last day at *Marlag und Milag Nord*. By all that was fair and right, he should have been sitting down with the rest of us, composing his own "glad tidings" telegram.

Cablegrams handed in, we were assembled in a study hall to be briefed by a Canadian colonel on what was coming next. He pointed out that it would be months before our pay records and any other service data could be assembled. However, it was obvi-ous we all had at least four months of accumulated back pay coming. If we would sign receipts for pay advances, indicating our name, rank, regiment, and army serial number, we would be advanced twenty dollars a night while we were in Brussels, up to a maximum of three nights. He was sure we would be out of Brussels in three days' time. He surmised that after months, or years, of enforced celibacy, many of us would be inclined to go "out on the town." He assured us there was no shortage of ready, willing, and able Belgian girls eager to help us celebrate. We were big boys, and he was far from being a member of the chaplain's corps, though he felt he should point out that social diseases were rampant. It would be all too easy to bring home painful and totally unwanted souvenirs of Brussels.

Drawing my twenty dollars' equivalency in AMGOT (Allied Military Government for Occupied Territories) Belgian francs, I teamed up with a newfound buddy, Jeff Thompson from Waco, Texas. We set out to explore Brussels. It was a large and exciting city. As the colonel had said, the girls were not shy, and no one need sleep alone who didn't really want to.

On every hand flew homemade yellow-black-and-red striped Belgian flags. Novelty stores were doing a brisk business in miniature clotheslines, complete with tiny garments and pegs, bearing the slogan, "We're hanging out our washing on the Siegfried Line."

Sure enough, the Canadian colonel was right about how quickly we would transit through Brussels. The next morning, about eleven o'clock, we were assembled and trucked out to a nearby airfield to be flown to the giant U.S. staging area, Camp Lucky Strike in Le Havre, France. Once again, this was another combat aircraft, a Wellington, diverted from bombing duties for a few hours on a humanitarian mission to speed some RAMPs on their homeward way. We all sat down again on the floor of the bomb bay, though this time there were cross braces and ribs between the girders, so we could brace our feet and stay reasonably well in one place. We were all pretty blasé about flying, now that we were making our second flight in as many days.

Camp Lucky Strike was an all-American operation, and it was vast. An isolated incident I recall vividly was the truck ride from the Le Havre airstrip to the camp reception center. A fellow from Georgia was driving the truck, and he could really wheel it along. Somehow, somewhere, he had acquired a small brown-and-white beagle crossbreed that he had trained to ride on the truck hood like a living hood ornament. With the truck barreling along at forty-plus miles an hour over a bumpy, cobbled road, the dog would shift his weight like an expert water skier or a high-wire artist as the truck swerved first to the right and then to the left. The driver was sure proud of that dog. Gold teeth glistening in a broad smile, he rewarded the dog with biscuits and a chocolate bar at the end of the run.

After we had checked in and been assigned tents, we were assembled to hear what the future had in store for us. Wishing us well, the camp commander outlined the acute transportation situation. There was a real shortage of shipping space. Boys went back to the States on a fixed priority rotation. The badly wounded, of course, went first, and the walking wounded were second. Fighting detachments headed for the Pacific had obvious priority. Recovered prisoners were well up on the list, but with the heavy demands and sharply curtailed shipping space, it would be a considerable time before we could expect to be on our way home.

I believe he even added up ships available, calculated their troop-carrying capabilities, and told us to bargain on a full eight weeks before we could expect to embark. Within the camp, it was a "first come, first served" policy, and we were just about the last of the last to be liberated.

That very evening at Lucky Strike, I ran into the Mexican-American sergeant from *Stalag* X B. He was still the custodian of the Argentinian brigade and was at that very moment en route to camp headquarters to try to explain this fantastic tale to the camp authorities. He pounced on me like a lost brother, and nothing else would do but that I accompany him to the colonel's office to substantiate a story that needed substantiation, if ever a story did.

The colonel heard us out in openmouthed wonder. While I stayed there, the sergeant was dispatched to fetch the two principals in the case. I readily testified that these were the same two men whom I had met while a prisoner at Sandbostel and identified two tiny facsimiles of Argentine flags that they had sewn inside their shirtsleeves. This was certainly a problem not covered in the military manual. When all the data had been taken down and recorded, the colonel went off into a series of questions that the sergeant duly submitted to Sanchez and Co., and the answers were transcribed.

When I next saw the sergeant, some three days later, he was grinning like a Cheshire cat. The top camp authorities had decided that if two Argentinians were sufficiently devoted to the cause of freedom to roam the world for nine years to fight for it, the least Uncle Sam could do was to give them a free boat ride. The arrangement, at that time, was that they were to be put off in a pilot boat and land at Ellis Island. The Argentine consul at New York had been notified. Unless Peron chose to send up a gunboat, I suppose their respective families raised the passage money for the last leg of this strange odyssey, the voyage from Ellis Island to Buenos Aires. Even if they didn't, I am sure these two boys would have found a way to make it on their own.

Faced with a minimum of two months loafing at Camp Lucky Strike, I had a sudden brainstorm. I had been born in Penryn, Cornwall, England, a scant ninety miles across the English Channel from Le Havre. It seemed very unlikely that I would ever be in this part of the world again. These factors made it seem both logical and sensible that I should make an effort to see my relatives: two aunts, an uncle, and two cousins. I had a particularly strong desire to see the house where I had been born. I certainly was not jeopardizing anything, as I had been told, straight out, that it would be an absolute minimum of eight weeks before I could hope to board a vessel for the U.S. Retracing my steps, I returned to camp headquarters to request an English furlough. The lieutenant I spoke to had been in on the Argentinian interrogation. He recognized me, and I'm sure this helped me get a quick OK for a furlough not to exceed three weeks in duration.

I was given a requisition to draw needed new clothing and a pass to enable me to make my way to Saint-Valery-sur-Somme, where I was to pick up a lift on one of the dozens of small craft that shuttled back and forth across the Channel daily. At the quartermaster building, I requisitioned new shoes, shirt, pants, and jacket. I remember the amazement and scorn of the issuing GI corporal because I hadn't asked for a raincoat. According to him, the raincoat should have been the very top item on my little list. Anyone foolishly going to England without a raincoat was "out of his cotton-picking mind." Bowing to his superior knowledge of the vagaries of English weather, I humbly took the raincoat.

This was to be a two-man travel party. I was to go with Pvt. Norman Clarke, from Worcester, Massachusetts, who had a burning desire to see his girlfriend in Northampton, England. I'm sure that for the purpose of obtaining the furlough, it was far more expedient for him to identify his girlfriend, a nurse, as his "cousin."

I well remember the travel orders cut in seventy-four copies with voluminous distribution to Mediterranean Base Sector Command, SHAEF in London, RAMP headquarters in Brussels, and further copies to Washington and a dozen other filing cabinets around the world. All this to record a short furlough trip for PFC Clarke, group leader, and Private Dower, who was the "group." It sounds ludicrous, but it was true.

On May 8, 1945, we left Le Havre on a train that chugged along northward to Saint-Valery-sur-Somme, giving us glimpses of the gray-blue Channel on our left as it passed through French seaside villages and the city of Dieppe. Checking along the dock area, we were able to get passage on a small coastal craft leaving for Southampton within the hour. It seemed that good fortune was smiling on our venture all the way.

CHAPTER 26

The House Where I Was Born

O ur two-man travel group landed in Southampton about 5:00 P.M. on May 8. The city was delirious. Hundreds of church bells were ringing, people were dancing in the streets, and everyone in uniform was being embraced: It was V-E Day! Amazingly enough, there was NOT A DROP TO DRINK IN THE PUBS. As a matter of fact, the pubs were closed. Any liquid stocks previously on hand had apparently been drunk up in anticipation a day or two earlier.

Making my way to the train station, it soon became clear that fares were an unneeded frivolity in England that day, for people in uniform at any rate. You found a train going your way and just climbed aboard. To wear any uniform was ticket enough. If you were lucky, you hit a compartment filled with WAAF (Women's Auxiliary Air Force), NAAFI, ATS (Auxiliary Territorial Service), or Land Army girls. No matter how prudish or shy they might normally have been, all were lavish with their kisses on V-E Day, and for some, kissing was only the beginning of their generosity.

I had just enough time for a hasty few words with Norm Clarke. We exchanged addresses where we could contact each other by phone or telegram. Coming over on the boat, I had skimmed through our seventy-four-copy travel orders and found a flaw. They said that our granted furlough in England was not to exceed three weeks after the date the boat landed. No one knew which boat we arrived on. As long as we stuck to our stories, we could claim it took us several days or even a week in Saint-Valery-sur-Somme to secure steamer space. I guess this bears out the old truism, "There is a little larceny in every man's heart."

Most Southampton rail travelers, including Norm Clarke, were heading for London. In studying the station platform map, checking a Southern Railways timetable, and talking with a porter, it became apparent that I would be bucking the usual trend. I had a real journey ahead of me, with changes at Salisbury, Exeter, Plymouth, and Truro.

Exeter was as far as I got that night. Exeter was the city where you had to make your way from one railway station to another; Exeter Central Station was a mile removed from Exeter St. David's Station. In between the two was a cozy youth hostel sort of place that seemed to cater primarily to wandering GIs. For a couple of shillings, they provided you with a nice clean place to bed down, plus a solid bacon-and-egg breakfast to speed the traveler on his way the next morning.

Toting my kit bag, neatly turned out in my brand-new uniform and smart Eisenhower jacket, I was off again, bright and early, on the train to Plymouth and then to Truro. The Truro branch line ended in Falmouth, the home of my Aunt Mary and Uncle Will.

Unheralded, unanticipated, and totally unexpected, I climbed out of a taxi in front of a very pretty bungalow and presented myself at Aunt Mary's front door at 3:00 P.M., May 9.

As she swung open the door, I saw her facial resemblance to my mother, and she intuitively knew who I was. My mother was one of four sisters. Ada and Beatrice had emigrated to America right after World War I, settling in the Hartford, Connecticut, area, while sisters Mary and Nell had remained in Cornwall. Every week, each sister sent long, detailed letters to the two across the seas. The weekly newspaper, the *Falmouth Packet*, was read in our house with vastly more interest than the local *Hartford Times*. Snapshots frequently went back and forth across the Atlantic. I had a good mental picture of my Aunt Mary, Aunt Nell, and cousins Gerald and Percy. Mary's husband, Will, and my cousin Gerald came running across the street from their garage in seconds. A message was immediately phoned to a neighbor of my Aunt Nell in the adjacent small town of Penryn, two miles away. Aunt Nell joined us for supper that evening. How little did I realize then that inadvertently she would have a great hand in shaping my future destiny.

Reflecting now, I recall that the weather had been perfect ever since my *Marlag und Milag Nord* liberation. We had brilliant sunshine in Diepholz, Hannover, Brussels, Le Havre, Southampton, and now Falmouth and Penryn. The quartermaster's grim comments about gray, drizzly, cold English rain seemed absurd. Perhaps God was celebrating the end of the carnage and making His pleasure manifest with superb weather.

That sure was a happy supper at Dracaena Avenue, Falmouth, with Uncle Will slicing the meat, Aunt Mary bustling back and forth from the kitchen, and Aunt Nell and cousin Gerald plying me with a stream of questions. Aunt Nell was a truly remarkable woman. She was a member of a wholly selfless band, devoted to serving humanity, whose like I'm convinced will never be seen again. A spinster of sixty-five, Nell was short and stocky with a red, snub-nosed, Winston Churchill–type face. She invariably wore her navy blue visiting nurse uniform, complete with Sam Browne belt and navy blue broad-brimmed campaign hat. She was loved and respected by all.

Every day, rain or shine, she patrolled her district, which took in a radius of four or five miles, on her trusty bicycle. Lashed to a carrier platform behind the bicycle seat was the battered brown leather surgical bag with her instruments, thermometers, anesthetics, suppositories, lotions, bandages, poultices, syrups, laxatives, scissors, and pills. Crammed into that fairly small bag was a veritable rolling hospital. In her kindly, tireless body and mind was a store of knowledge built up over a forty-six-year career of nursing, initially in London hospitals but over the past thirty years dedicated to her Penryn neighbors as their beloved "Nurse Spargo."

Breech births, setting broken limbs, cutting old-age pensioners' toenails, croup, diarrhea, pleurisy, diphtheria, phlebitis, you name it. Nurse Spargo diagnosed, prescribed, and cared for all the sick and infirm in her district. Nell and her colleagues had literally lived the Florence Nightingale legend, as any local doctor would gladly attest. She seemed to thrive on pushing her bicycle up steep hills and splashing along unpaved country lanes, making her ministering rounds. At every stop she was offered homemade buns and cups of tea, and she acted as the willing or unwilling confidante of hundreds of patients. Nell was truly loved by all.

There was no subtlety to Aunt Nell. She told it like it was. Nell had scant sympathy for hurt feelings, protocol, and ceremony. There were more important things going on.

It must have been May 11 when I was standing with Aunt Nell directly across from 97 West Street, Penryn, a low granite building fronting directly on a granite sidewalk that must have been all of twenty inches wide. Nell was saying, "Yes, Jack, that's the house you were born in, right in the upstairs bedroom. I remember it well. You came out all wrinkled and red and screeching just a few seconds after you arrived."

At that moment, the door of 97 West Street opened. A young girl stepped out. "Sylvia, Sylvia," called Nell. "Come over here and meet my nephew from America." The road couldn't have been any more than fifteen feet wide, but Sylvia could have heard Nell's booming, drill sergeant voice if she was in the next county. As she came across the narrow roadway, I thought to myself what a pretty girl she was.

Ever direct, even to the point of bluntness, Nell spoke up. "Sylvia, my girl, isn't there a dance going on somewhere that you can take Jack to? He has more than earned some relaxation, and I'm expecting you to see to it that he enjoys his stay in Penryn." Poor Sylvia must have been mightily embarrassed at Nell's directness, but she put the best face on the situation. Blushing more than a little, she replied, "Why yes, there is a dance tonight at the Princess Pavilion. If Jack would like to go, I'd be glad to have him come with me. Betty Hodge, Betty Medlyn, and lots of the other girls will be there, and there will be a first-rate band."

I was embarrassed for Sylvia. I was going to the dance by directive, almost by ultimatum. This was a command performance if ever there was one.

The date set, Nell and I went a few feet down West Street to her little house. With the teakettle furiously boiling away, and puffing on her cigarette, Nell told me that I had been born in the upstairs bedroom at 97 West Street on May 3, 1919. The following February, my folks sold their little grocery store with the living quarters directly overhead and immigrated to America.

The people who purchased the premises had remained only two or three years, and then the property had been sold to Alf and Kate Thomas. The young girl who was to take me to the dance that evening was Sylvia Thomas, the youngest of Alf's three daughters. Coincidentally, Sylvia had also been born in that same upstairs bedroom. Nell figured that Sylvia was about twenty, so that would have put her birth year about 1925. Nell hastened to reassure me that all births were in modern hospitals now, but midwifery was not all that uncommon in rural Cornwall as late as 1930.

Right on time, at seven o'clock, I crossed the street and met Alf and Kate Thomas and their second daughter, Honorine. Alf and Kate remembered my parents well. After the usual pleasantries, we set off for the Princess Pavilion and the Victory Dance. My dancing was never very expert, and in army boots I must have been a real menace on the dance floor. The band belted out the familiar Glenn Miller tunes with enthusiasm, if not expertise. It was a swell evening for me; I even won a prize. There was a spotlight dance, and if you were on the right spot at the right time, you won. I can recall that the band stopped in midbeat, the spotlight came on, there was a roll of the drums, a little Cub Scout marched out, gave me a very military salute, and presented me with a tin of fifty Senior Service cigarettes. In retrospect, I'm positive the contest was rigged. I was probably the only person in Cornwall at that time in American uniform. To be an American in grateful Britain, just after V-E Day, was to be on the very pinnacle. I was in the right place, at the right time, in more ways than one.

During intermission Sylvia introduced me to her many friends, and we had cakes and buns and innumerable cups of tea. There were quite a few older people at the dance, and many of them remembered my parents. To be an American was unusual enough, but to be a Penryn-born American, and a nephew of Nurse Spargo, was to be a celebrity indeed.

The town was staging a victory parade on Saturday. The mayor, all decked out in his chains of office, asked if I would march and represent the United States. "Of course, I'd be glad to march in your parade." After slogging almost a thousand miles in ice and snow across northern Germany, the prospect of a one-mile parade in Penryn didn't sound very daunting.

The Princess Pavilion dance was followed by a dance an evening or two later at the Central Services Hall in Falmouth. After that came a day's outing with Sylvia to the lovely seaside town of St. Ives, where we visited Bill Veal, one of my *Marlag und Milag Nord* buddies, who had returned home just a few days before I got to Cornwall.

By this time, I was captivated by the charming Sylvia, but this was a captivity that I welcomed. Romance blossomed. In a short week or two, I knew that my decision to visit Penryn to see the house where I was born had been a fateful one. I proposed one afternoon on the sea cliffs above St. Ives, looking down on the sparkling blue Bristol Channel. Sylvia was elated and quickly said yes, but this was Elizabethan Cornwall, and I would have to present my case and secure Alf Thomas's blessing or it would be "all off." Sylvia was a dutiful daughter. If dad didn't come through with the parental blessing, there would be no wedding bells. Fortunately, I passed muster. I don't attribute this to my boyish charm. I feel sure Alf approved mainly because I was Nurse Spargo's nephew and the Thomases knew my mother and dad.

Engaged, I sailed for home. Sylvia came to America the following year, and on November 23, 1946, we were married in Stamford, Connecticut. The two people who had been born in the upstairs bedroom at 97 West Street, Penryn, Cornwall, were now Mr. and Mrs. Jack Dower of Hartford, Connecticut.

Epilogue

After returning to Connecticut and marrying his Cornish beauty, Sylvia, in 1946, Jack Dower embarked on a marketing and exporting career that was capped with receiving the prestigious "E" Award from the U.S. Department of Commerce. He was active on the zoning committee in the small town of Burlington, and always enjoyed telling the story of when he ran for office to be a local justice of the peace. His rival, knowing that Sylvia was not yet a citizen, used the campaign slogan, "Even my opponent's *own wife* won't vote for him!"

Most evenings, Jack sat at the kitchen table, hunting and pecking on his Underwood typewriter to compose this book. He never talked about the war and carefully put the manuscript away each night.

Jack was a familiar face at the local library, where he regularly exhausted the nonfiction section as well as the Robert Benchley and P. G. Wodehouse stock. Weekends usually found him on the golf course sporting a pair of pants Sylvia wouldn't let him wear anywhere else. His two holes-in-one were a point of quiet pride.

A lifelong Republican, Jack was delighted when his daughter Susan moved to Washington, D.C., and took a job on Capitol Hill. Attending President Ronald Reagan's first inauguration was a true highlight in his life, but sadly he did not get to attend the second one. On an August 1984 trip to revisit the scene of his Benzin internment, Pvt. Jack Dower succumbed to a sudden massive heart attack. *(Courtesy of Susan A. Carleson, daughter of Jack Dower)*

BORN IN MANHATTAN, LT. JAMES F. CALLAHAN ("Lieutenant") grew up the oldest of four children in the Bronx. After helping to build the Tennessee Valley Dam with the Civil Conservation Corps, he joined the U.S. Army and was stationed in Hawaii until 1938. Jim then took a brief break from service, but when America joined the war effort, he reenlisted in February 1942.

Jim was leading Company L when it was captured at Anzio. The Germans had a strict policy of separating officers and enlisted prisoners, so while his troops traveled to their destination in one train, he traveled in another, ultimately ending up at *Oflag* 64, in Szubin, Poland.

Following his marriage to Maria Sadowski in 1945, he was reassigned overseas. Finally, in 1947, Jim left the army, returning to his prewar employer, Breyers, and settling down to build a fine family of five children, all of whom, luckily, shared an affection for ice cream.

Jim retired with Maria to the countryside in New Fairfield, Connecticut, in 1967 to enjoy life with his grandchildren. He was an avid collector of stamps, coins, and artifacts, and his love of nature and photography led to a successful avocation as an artist. His oil paintings grace many homes across the country.

Sadly, after fifty-three years of marriage, cancer took the life of Lt. James F. Callahan on March 28, 1998. *(Courtesy of Patricia Bowers, daughter of James Callahan)*

A FIRST-GENERATION AMERICAN, JOHNNY DICRECCHIO was the only surviving son of Italian parents, who landed on Ellis Island in 1919. He was still attending Portland High when the war broke out, and when he heard the news, he headed straight down to the navy recruitment office. However, he wasn't tall enough, so he joined the army instead.

In the spring of 1950, his sister Gilda played matchmaker and introduced Johnny to a pretty workmate named Lois Smith. It was love at first sight, and the wedding was held on October 29, 1951, at Portland's First Universalist Church. The happy couple was blessed with two daughters, Anita and Denise.

Johnny was only twenty years old when he finally saw the end of his POW days in 1945. The experience of war left many scars, and the effects of malnutrition and the harsh memories of his imprisonment remained with Johnny throughout his life. After many years of medication and electric shock therapy at the veteran's hospital in Togus, Maine, he was able to return home.

Thankfully, Johnny had married a strong and courageous woman who kept the family together while he was gone. He loved to serenade Lois with his favorite song lyric: "Put another nickel in, in the Nickelodeon, all I want is loving you and music, music, music."

Sadly, the music stopped on October 28, 1976, when congestive heart failure took Johnny's life. Johnny DiCrecchio was a patriot of the first order. He did his duty to God, his country, and his family. While he didn't live to see the first of his six grandchild born, he did know that his granddaughter Kelly was on the way. *(Courtesy of Anita DiCrecchio, daughter of John DiCrecchio)*

NICHOLAS F. D'ERRICO JR. was born and raised in New Haven, Connecticut, and like his siblings, he found an early love for music. When he was not busy working as a clothing salesman, an automobile salesman, volunteer firefighter, or school custodian, he could be found in a club or at a private affair joining a local band on the drums.

Following the war, Nick returned home to marry Jean Russo and began playing professionally with several area bands. He was proud of the fact that he once performed before President Ronald Reagan. Nick passed his love for drums on to his son, Nicholas D'Errico III, and his grandson, Nick D'Errico IV, who today follows in his grandfather's footsteps and can be heard playing at events throughout the Hartford area.

Nick worked hard at everything he did and was blessed with a very loving and close-knit family life. His relatives were so important to him that in the 1960s he began a tradition of organizing regular family reunions. They are not the same without him.

Nick D'Errico Jr., beloved by so many, passed away from cardiac arrest on June 7, 2006, at the age of eighty-one. *(Special thanks to Florence D'Errico, daughter-in-law of Nicholas D'Errico Jr.)*

JESSE MCDONALD suffered from the brutal forced march across Germany in the winter of 1944. Despite his best efforts to keep warm, he developed a bad case of frostbite on his hands and feet—so bad, in fact, that he was pulled out of the line and transported to a prison hospital near New Brandenburg. It was there that the Russians set him free on the morning of April 29, 1945.

Born and raised in Michigan, Jesse entered Lawrence Technical University upon returning to Detroit. When he wasn't hitting the books or a golf ball, he held a part-time job at Crowley's Department Store. One day, while he was in the cafeteria line to get a root beer float, he met fellow employee Martha Kremer. It was love at first sip, and they got married in August 1949.

Jesse graduated from Lawrence in 1951 with a degree in civil engineering and soon went on to become a star in his profession. He's responsible for the construction of a number of important buildings around the country, including the corporate headquarters for Playtex Bras.

Through the years Jesse and Martha were blessed with five sons and five grandchildren. Always an extraordinary golfer, even holding the #1 rank on his team at school, Jesse can still be found most mornings teeing up on his favorite course. *(Courtesy of Jesse and Martha McDonald)*

RAYMOND J. KUDLOSKI was born and raised in Detroit, Michigan, in 1923. Following the tragic early death of his brother, he grew up as an only child. He was drafted into the army shortly after the U.S. entered World War II. Ray didn't waste time following his release as a POW. Upon returning to Detroit, he married Wanda Kossak, and they had two sons, Leonard and Gregory.

Ray was a career businessman. He started off by purchasing a bar, then tried his hand at owning a resort in Indian River, Michigan. That turned out to be a short-lived venture, but Ray then found his stride as an owner of a Kowalski's Grocery Store, the home of the famous "Kowalski Bratski," a staple of the American 1960s.

Tragically, at the young age of thirty-six, Ray suffered a major heart attack on the Fourth of July. He never recovered, and his health continued to fail until his untimely passing two years later at the veteran's hospital in Allen Park, Michigan, on October 22, 1961. *(Special thanks to Gregory and Leonard Kudloski, sons of Raymond Kudloski)*

JOHN ERNEST BENSON was born on May 3, 1923, in Chicago, Illinois, and spent all of his youth there. Following the war, he met and married his wife, Agnes, and became the father of two stepchildren. The family later moved to San Diego, where John became a devout follower of Buddhism. By all accounts, John was a very patient man, known by those closest to him to always be of an even temper.

John became an aerospace engineer and for thirty-nine years was employed by the spacecraft pioneering company Convair. He was proud of his career and the fact that he worked on several important projects, including the Atlas missile program.

Sadly, at the end of a battle with Alzheimer's disease, John passed on May 20, 2010, at the age of eighty-seven. *(Special thanks to Sachiko Held, stepdaughter of John Benson)*

VERNON "OLE" OLSON ("SWEDE") was born in Antigo, Wisconsin, in 1911 and spent his life there except for a few unwelcomed years as a guest of the Nazis. He was always an honest, hard-working man, and from an early age, he and his brother enjoyed woodworking, log-sawing, and pulp-cutting.

Following the war, Vernon tried his hand as a butcher, but didn't like it. His love for the outdoors was too strong, so he went to work for his brother at Olson's Balsams, a tree farm in Antigo. To this day, Vernon's nephew Duane Olson carries on the family tradition by providing the perfect Christmas trees to families far and wide. Vernon was a quiet man of few words, but according to Duane, "he was always willing to argue about how to cut a log."

Vernon suffered from the effects of POW life, but even as he was struggling with his health, he showed up faithfully to work with his brother, until one day in 1961, at age fifty, when he succumbed to a heart attack. *(Special thanks to Duane Olson, nephew of Vernon Olson)*

JOHN ANDREW ESTOCK, the oldest of six children, grew up in a small community called "The Patch." In his teens, he helped his steel-worker father support the family after they moved to Clairton, Pennsylvania, the "City of Prayer" featured in the iconic film *The Deer Hunter.*

John had been drafted into the army and was very proud that his two brothers and oldest sister served alongside him. On his return from the war, John met and fell in love with Mildred Mihock, and they married in October 1945. The couple moved to a small ranch house in nearby Glasport and over the years raised three daughters.

John followed in his father's footsteps in the steel industry and was employed by the Clarion Works until his retirement in May 1976. When he wasn't at his job, John enjoyed gardening, long walks, crossword puzzles, and playing polkas on his accordion.

Sadly, John's retirement was very short-lived, and he passed in October 1976 at the age of sixty-four. *(Special thanks to Pat Vorkapich, daughter of John Estock)*

ARCHIE RAY BLEVINS was a proud Beckley, West Virginia boy, the third of six children. His older sister recalls that he was an outgoing youngster who declared he was smarter than his teacher when he quit school in the seventh grade. After working at a number of odd jobs, Archie joined the army on May 3, 1943.

When he returned home from the war, Archie didn't talk about his experience. He went from being full of life to a quiet and religious man who loved studying the Bible. Always with a smile on his face and a whistle on his lips, it wasn't long before he met and married the young and lovely Louise McKinney.

Archie worked in the local coal mines until 1952, but when he was laid off, he and Louise moved to Michigan, where he got a job at Great Lakes Steel. Their growing family of six children required that Archie work two jobs to make ends meet.

Tragically, in 1973 Archie was diagnosed with tuberculosis. The doctors believed he contracted the disease when he was a POW, and after a two-year stay at the Herman Kiefer Hospital, Archie lost half his left lung. The dreadful disease affected the whole family, and after testing positive, son Ronnie, who was only five years old, had to be hospitalized for six months.

A year later, Archie retired from Great Lakes Steel. He and Louise and their youngest child returned to West Virginia for the good mountain air. A close family, they made many trips back to Michigan to visit their other five children, who were grown with families of their own. Sadly, on October 28, 2001, Archie, with Louise at his side, succumbed to cancer. *(Courtesy of Shirley Lewis, daughter of Archie Blevins)*

ELMER MORGAN EAGLE was born on August 2, 1922, in Droop Mountain, West Virginia, the site of the state's last major conflict of the Civil War. He grew up in the incredibly scenic country of the Falls of Hills Creek and what is now Beartown State Park on the eastern summit of the mountain.

Elmer was drafted into the army, and when he returned home and married, he lived a simple life as a farmer, never moving more than fifteen miles from where he had been born. He regretted not going to school when he came out of the service, but he could never leave his beloved country life.

Elmer was a devoted father of four and a renowned vegetable gardener. He had a passion for the outdoors and always said that "when his time came" he wanted go while either hunting or fishing. He got his wish. On October 14, 1992, while hunting with one of his sons, he passed from a heart attack. *(Special thanks to Chris Eagle, grandson of Elmer Eagle)*

DELBERT LEE KINDER was born in Morehead, Kentucky, on July 13, 1923. Orphaned as a young boy, he moved to his aunt and uncle's farm, where he learned to raise tobacco.

Delbert, the father of three, wed Georgia Andrew in 1968. They were married for thirty-eight years and had five children together. During most of that time, Delbert worked as a printer for the Dayton Legal Blank Company in Dayton, Ohio.

In addition to his job, Delbert had a passion for ministering to others. He faithfully served for forty-five years as a minister, most recently for the congregation of Chapel Baptist Church in Dayton. Delbert passed away on September 17, 2006, at the age of eighty-three.

Stackpole Military History Series

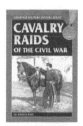
CAVALRY RAIDS OF THE CIVIL WAR

IN THE LION'S MOUTH
Hood's Tragic Retreat from Nashville, 1864

WITNESS TO GETTYSBURG
Inside the Battle That Changed the Course of the Civil War

DOUGHBOY WAR
The American Expeditionary Force in WWI

AFTER D-DAY
Operation Cobra and the Normandy Breakout

AIRBORNE COMBAT
The Glider War / Fighting Gliders of WWII

ARMOR BATTLES OF THE WAFFEN SS 1943–45

ARMOURED GUARDSMEN
A War Diary from Normandy to the Rhine

ARNHEM 1944
The Airborne Battle

B-24 IN CHINA
General Chennault's Secret Weapon in WWII

THE BATTALION
The Dramatic Story of the 2nd Ranger Battalion in WWII

THE BATTLE OF FRANCE
Six Weeks That Changed the World

THE BATTLE OF SICILY
How the Allies Lost Their Chance for Total Victory

BATTLE OF THE BULGE
Volume One: The Losheim Gap / Holding the Line

BATTLE OF THE BULGE
Volume Two: Bell at Büllingen / Seize the Bridges

BATTLE OF THE BULGE
Volume Three: The 3rd Fallschirmjäger in Action, December 1944–January 1945

BEYOND THE BEACHHEAD
The 29th Infantry Division in Normandy

BEYOND STALINGRAD
Manstein and the Operations of Army Group Don

BLACK BULL
From Normandy to the Baltic with the 11th Armoured Division

BLITZKRIEG UNLEASHED
The German Invasion of Poland, 1939

BLOSSOMING SILK AGAINST THE RISING SUN
U.S. and Japanese Paratroopers at War in the Pacific in WWII

BODENPLATTE
The Luftwaffe's Last Hope

BREAKING POINT
Sedan and the Fall of France, 1940

THE BRIGADE
The Fifth Canadian Infantry Brigade in WWII

CANADIAN ARMY AND THE NORMANDY CAMPAIGN

CLAY PIGEONS OF ST. LÔ

CRITICAL CONVOY BATTLES OF WWII
Crisis in the North Atlantic, March 1943

DANGEROUS ASSIGNMENT
An Artillery Forward Observer in WWII

D-DAY BOMBERS
The Stories of Allied Heavy Bombers during the Invasion of Normandy

D-DAY DECEPTION
Operation Fortitude and the Normandy Invasion

Real battles. Real soldiers. Real stories.

D-DAY TO BERLIN
The Northwest Europe Campaign, 1944–45

DECISION IN THE UKRAINE
German Panzer Operations on the Eastern Front, Summer 1943

THE DEFENSE OF MOSCOW 1941
The Northern Flank

DELIVERANCE AT DIEPHOLZ
A WWII Prisoner of War's Story

DESTINATION NORMANDY
Three American Regiments on D-Day

DIVE BOMBER!
Aircraft, Technology, and Tactics in WWII

EAGER EAGLES
The U.S. Eighth Air Force in Europe, 1941–43

EAGLES OF THE THIRD REICH
Men of the Luftwaffe in WWII

THE EARLY BATTLES OF EIGHTH ARMY
Crusader to the Alamein Line, 1941–42

EASTERN FRONT COMBAT
The German Soldier in Battle from Stalingrad to Berlin

EUROPE IN FLAMES
Understanding WWII

EXIT ROMMEL
The Tunisian Campaign, 1942–43

THE FACE OF COURAGE

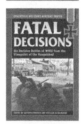
FATAL DECISIONS
Six Decisive Battles of WWII from the Viewpoint of the Vanquished

FIST FROM THE SKY
Japan's Dive-Bomber Ace of WWII

FLAME ON
U.S. Incendiary Weapons, 1918–1945

FLYING AMERICAN COMBAT AIRCRAFT OF WWII
1939–45

FOR EUROPE
The French Volunteers of the Waffen-SS

FORGING THE THUNDERBOLT
History of the US Army's Armored Forces, 1917–45

FOR THE HOMELAND
The 31st Waffen-SS Volunteer Grenadier Division in WWII

FORTRESS FRANCE
The Maginot Line and French Defenses in WWII

GERMAN DEFEAT IN THE EAST
1944–45

GERMAN ORDER OF BATTLE
Volume One: 1st–290th Infantry Divisions in WWII

GERMAN ORDER OF BATTLE
Volume Two: 291st–999th Infantry Divisions, Named Infantry Divisions, and Special Divisions in WWII

GERMAN ORDER OF BATTLE
Volume Three: Panzer, Panzer Grenadier, and Waffen-SS Divisions in WWII

THE GERMANS IN NORMANDY

GERMANY'S PANZER ARM IN WWII

GI INGENUITY
Improvisation, Technology, and Winning WWII

GOODBYE, TRANSYLVANIA
A Romanian Waffen-SS Soldier in WWII

THE GREAT SHIPS
British Battleships in WWII

Stackpole Military History Series

 GRENADIERS

 GUNS AGAINST THE REICH

 HITLER'S FINAL FORTRESS

 HITLER'S NEMESIS

 HITLER'S SPANISH LEGION

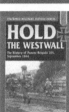 HOLD THE WESTWALL

 INFANTRY ACES

 IN THE FIRE OF THE EASTERN FRONT

 IRON ARM

 IRON KNIGHTS

 JAPANESE ARMY FIGHTER ACES

 JAPANESE NAVAL FIGHTER ACES

 JG 26 LUFTWAFFE FIGHTER WING WAR DIARY Volume One: 1939–42

 JG 26 LUFTWAFFE FIGHTER WING WAR DIARY Volume Two: 1943–45

 KAMPFGRUPPE PEIPER AT THE BATTLE OF THE BULGE

 THE KEY TO THE BULGE

 KURSK

 LUFTWAFFE ACES

 LUFTWAFFE FIGHTER ACE

 LUFTWAFFE FIGHTER-BOMBERS OVER BRITAIN

 LUFTWAFFE FIGHTERS & BOMBERS

 LUFTWAFFE KG 200

 MARSHAL OF VICTORY

 MARSHAL OF VICTORY

 MASSACRE AT TOBRUK

 MECHANIZED JUGGERNAUT OR MILITARY ANACHRONISM?

 MESSERSCHMITTS OVER SICILY

 MICHAEL WITTMANN VOLUME ONE

 MICHAEL WITTMANN VOLUME TWO

 MISSION 85

Real battles. Real soldiers. Real stories.

Stackpole Military History Series

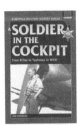
SOLDIER IN THE COCKPIT
From Rifles to Typhoons in WWII

SOVIET BLITZKRIEG
The Battle for White Russia, 1944

SPITFIRES & YELLOW TAIL MUSTANGS
The U.S. 52nd Fighter Group in WWII

STALIN'S KEYS TO VICTORY
The Rebirth of the Red Army in WWII

SURVIVING BATAAN AND BEYOND
Colonel Irvin Alexander's Odyssey as a Japanese Prisoner of War

T-34 IN ACTION
Soviet Tank Troops in WWII

TANK TACTICS
From Normandy to Lorraine

TIGERS IN THE MUD
The Combat Career of German Panzer Commander Otto Carius

TRIUMPHANT FOX
Erwin Rommel and the Rise of the Afrika Korps

THE 12TH SS
The History of the Hitler Youth Panzer Division: Volume One

THE 12TH SS
The History of the Hitler Youth Panzer Division: Volume Two

TWILIGHT OF THE GODS
A Swedish Volunteer in the 11th SS Panzergrenadier Division "Nordland" on the Eastern Front

TYPHOON ATTACK
The Legendary British Fighter in Combat in WWII

THE WAR AGAINST ROMMEL'S SUPPLY LINES
1942–43

WAR IN THE AEGEAN
The Campaign for the Eastern Mediterranean in WWII

WAR OF THE WHITE DEATH
Finland against the Soviet Union, 1939–40

WARSAW 1944
An Insurgent's Journal of the Uprising

WINTER STORM
The Battle for Stalingrad and the Operation to Rescue 6th Army

WINTER WAR
The Soviet Attack on Finland, 1939–1940

WOLFPACK WARRIORS
The Story of WWII's Most Successful Fighter Outfit

ZHUKOV AT THE ODER
The Decisive Battle for Berlin

CYCLOPS IN THE JUNGLE
A One-Eyed LRP in Vietnam

EXPENDABLE WARRIORS
The Battle of Khe Sanh and the Vietnam War

FIGHTING IN VIETNAM
The Experiences of the U.S. Soldier

FLYING AMERICAN COMBAT AIRCRAFT
The Cold War